BECOMING URBAN

THE MONGOLIAN CITY OF NOMADS

Joshua Bolchover

The expanse of the *ger* districts that house the majority of Ulaanbaatar's population.

CONTENTS

7   BECOMING URBAN

27 SETTLING THE NOMADS
    NOMADIC LIFE
    URBAN LIFE
    GER DISTRICT LIFE

73 PROTOTYPING
    BUILDING AS RESEARCH
    ADAPTIVE INFRASTRUCTURE
    ENABLING COMMUNITY
    TRANSFORMING AND UPGRADING THE GER

127 INCREMENTAL URBAN STRATEGY

141 INCREMENTAL DEVELOPMENT MANUAL

173 FRAMEWORK AS METHOD

186 ENDNOTES
190 CREDITS

BECO
MING

UR
BAN

The traditional nomadic ger becomes sedentary in the city.

BECOMING URBAN

For thousands of years, Mongolians have been living in *gers*—circular structures of timber and wool felt wrapped in stretched white canvas and pulled taught with horsehair rope. The ger is a highly evolved design object, easy to disassemble, move, and reassemble in a matter of hours without any tools or fixings. For these reasons it is a perfect dwelling for nomads who move up to 500 kilometers each year in search of seasonal pastures.[1] Historically, however, the ger has been a part of all forms of Mongolian settlements, urban or rural, and it remains the most affordable form of dwelling today.

Mongolia's 1990 democratic revolution and the subsequent collapse of Soviet state control precipitated a rapid rise in migration into the capital city of Ulaanbaatar, which saw its population increase 280 percent between 1989 and 2020[2] while its area extended to 35 times its original size.[3] The influx of people has resulted in the sprawl of settlements known as ger districts, which extend outward from the city, carpeting the valleys and hillsides with a mix of one- to two-story brick houses and traditional gers. This sprawl comprises thousands of individual plots, each surrounded with a two-meter-high fence (6.6 foot) wall made from wooden posts or salvaged metal. When walking the dirt roads of the districts, these barriers block views into each home, where typically a dog barks vociferously as you pass.

Occasional glimpses through cracks in the fences reveal traces of everyday life: car parts, scrap materials, kids' toys, old appliances, a shed, a wooden pit latrine.

None of the households in the ger districts have access to centrally supplied water, sewage, or district heating. Temperatures in Ulaanbaatar are below zero for over six months of the year, typically reaching -30°C (-22°F) in winter, and ger district residents burn coal and coke—the most readily available and affordable fuel—to keep warm. As a result, air pollution levels in the city are some of the worst in the world. Ger district dwellers have to collect water two or three times a day from water kiosks, bringing their own plastic one-gallon containers, filling them up, and then hauling them back to their homes, which can be up to a 30-minute walk, sometimes uphill and often on frozen, icy ground. Over 60 percent of the city's population lives in this way in the ger districts. The ger's affordability, portability, and reproducibility in large numbers—the characteristics that make it an ideal nomadic dwelling— have been a major contributing factor to the speed and extent of ger district growth in the city, and therefore also to the deleterious effects of this form of urban settlement.

The ger districts reflect a dystopian future world—a world still dependent on coal-based fossil fuels with an extreme climate, acrid air, polluted soils, and scarcity of water, where the population lives in unhealthy dwellings with a lack of civil and community resources. They offer a critical reflection on what might be unless we act upon the urgent issues of our time: climate change and income inequality, and their embodiment in the provision of sustainable, affordable homes. These extreme conditions are what first drew us to Ulaanbaatar seven years ago, to investigate and to test alternative models of architecture and urbanism. We have done this through built projects, spatial analysis, community engagement workshops, and intensive design-build construction events with teams of local people and students. Through the process we have developed an understanding of the pressures and difficulties facing residents, as well as those involved in urban policy and development, as the city and its population undergo a fundamental shift from a nomadic to a sedentary culture.

The ger's affordability, portability, and reproducibility in large numbers—the characteristics that make it an ideal nomadic dwelling—have been a major contributing factor to the speed and extent of ger district growth in the city.

In that shift, people face new problems they did not have to address as nomads. Space is parceled and owned, so negotiation is necessary in order to define borders between private and shared territories. Neighbors are often strangers from outside of family kinship networks, so common problems extend beyond the domestic domain and localized circles. The lack of sewage infrastructure in Ulaanbaatar's ger districts leads to compounding environmental degradation whereas its absence in the open territory of the steppe had almost no detrimental effects. Urban life furthermore requires an increased reliance on other entities to provide essential services such as electricity and waste collection. Tax, debt, and banks are new financial realities. Cash itself becomes an everyday necessity, while bartering sufficed on the nomadic steppe. Commodities such as a car, a house, or a TV articulate the stratification of society between the haves and the have-nots. No one lives in the same way as they did when they were nomads. In the process of this transformation, new problems together with new opportunities arise, so there becomes a need for collective decision-making and action.

How does this paradigmatic shift from a nomadic to a sedentary lifestyle take place? What spatial and organizational form does it take? What are the underlying mechanisms that shape this transformation? These questions are key to our investigations presented in this book, and their relevance extends well beyond Mongolia. The experience of Ulaanbaatar is an extreme example of what it means to become urban.

REALITY CHECK

If becoming urban is more than having access to employment, infrastructure, and a modernized dwelling, then how can it be defined and given spatial form through architecture? The seeming paradox of a city of nomads and of the creation of a permanent settlement for a traditionally nomadic culture is in fact a unique and fertile territory to explore what constitutes the urban realm today. Observing Mongolia allows us to critically reflect on how we live in the twenty-first century—a postindustrial, post-digital world where employment does not produce material things, trade operates through data analytics, algorithms determine behavior, social life is mediated and non-physical, and technological abstraction has disconnected us from the earth. Mongolia is a reality check, bringing heightened awareness to issues, such

No one lives in the same way as they did when they were nomads. In the process of this transformation, new problems together with new opportunities arise, so there becomes a need for collective decision-making and action.

The experience of Ulaanbaatar is an extreme example of what it means to become urban.

Technology has enabled our disassociation with the reality of the climate crisis. We hear about it and see images of it, but we don't feel it. It is an outside that is there, but to which we are becoming accustomed. And if there is a threat, it still feels elsewhere.

Fundamental questions of why we live together, how we collectively share resources, and the importance of community are raw and open to definition.

as the climate crisis, to which many of us have become habituated. Although the environment is the prevailing issue of this century that is fundamentally challenging contemporary ways of life, our responsibility and involvement in shaping this profound urgency has become diffused and displaced—it's not me, or us, but it's somewhere else and seemingly inevitable. Technology has enabled our disassociation with the reality of the climate crisis. We hear about it and see images of it, but we don't feel it. It is an outside that is there, but to which we are becoming accustomed. And if there is a threat, it still feels elsewhere.

In contrast, in the ger districts of Ulaanbaatar, the impact of the environmental crisis cannot be abstracted or mediated. It confronts you physically: the taste of the coal, the rasping of the lungs. The formation of these settlements and their continued expansion is worsening urban malaise and making it even more difficult to ameliorate living conditions. However, as the ger districts are in a state of emergence, there is a chance to change the trajectory of their development. Although the pressing need for access to infrastructure, heating, sewage, and sanitation is absolute, becoming urban is something more than problem-solving. Fundamental questions of why we live together, how we collectively share resources, and the importance of community are raw and open to definition. Each aspect needs to be addressed and given spatial form to articulate the direction of this ongoing urban transformation.

Even for established cities that have undergone centuries of sustained urbanization, such fundamental questions as why and how we live together and what it means to be a community are often taken for granted, and thus merit reassessment. Moreover, the larger forces underlying the processes of transformation in Mongolia—namely rural-to-urban migration, population relocation, the provision of affordable housing, and the environmental effects of urbanization—are key urgencies impacting cities in the developed and developing world alike. Consider the migration of more than 200 million people from rural to urban territory in India between 1990 and 2020,[4] or the relocation of populations brought about through infrastructural projects implemented to initiate urbanization and development in China, where it is estimated that 16 million citizens were rehoused between 2016 and 2020,[5] or the challenges of rural migration in Europe where, for example, 210,000 immigrants from rural origins migrated to German urban centers in 2020,[6] or the increased privatization of social housing that witnessed more than two million units privatised in England between 1980 and 2019.[7]

Simultaneously with the latter, the proportion of the cost of rent to income in England has increased from 16.8 percent to 45.5 percent over the last twenty years,[8] meaning that the cost of living in centrally located urban areas is unaffordable for most essential workers. Such lack of affordable housing is an escalating global issue, with reports estimating that the number of people living in substandard housing will increase from 330 million in 2014 to 1.6 billion by 2025.[9] As the world population becomes increasingly urbanized, estimated to reach 70 percent of the population by 2050,[10] the way cities are built and how we live in them will need to undergo systemic change to avoid the detrimental impacts of climate-related risks. The point is that these issues—migration, relocation, affordability, sustainability—are increasingly *the* critical issues being faced by urban cultures around the world.

Mongolia is particularly relevant to this discussion because it is grappling with some of the paradigmatic changes that shaped the twentieth century—namely, the shift from a communist state to a neoliberal, free-market democracy that occurred after the early 1990s with the fall of Soviet Union. Of the sixteen states that emerged from the USSR's collapse, only Mongolia, Estonia, Latvia, and Lithuania did not become dictatorships or controlled by oligarchs.[11] The shift in political and economic ideologies is visible in Ulaanbaatar's urban form, from the planned Soviet linear city and prefabricated apartment blocks to the developer-led commercial and hotel buildings such as Blue Sky, which appeared in 2010.

Mongolia is a country that seems to have missed its moment in terms of energy supply and natural resources. As much of the world is pledging to reduce carbon emissions to targets set by the 2016 Paris Accord, and China is stepping up its aim to reach net-zero emissions of carbon by 2060, Mongolia is mining the world's second largest coal deposit, discovered in 2001.[12] If Mongolia had been able to extract the coal when its commodity price was at its highest value, in 2008, it might have become an economically wealthy nation with a future more aligned with that of Norway, where the nation's resource wealth in the form of a rich supply of oil has been distributed to citizens through the Sovereign Pension Fund, established in 1990. However, the price of coal has decreased by 75 percent since its apex in 2008, reflecting a global shift away from coal due in part to its identification as a dirty fuel,[13] and thereby hindering any plans for similar accumulation in Mongolia.

In the ger districts of Ulaanbaatar, all of these issues stemming from Mongolia's political and economic history are brought to bear with heightened intensity and immediacy.

URBAN-RURAL TRENDS

The world has reached a tipping point since the 2007 UN declaration of an "urban age." Rapid urban growth rates in the developing world evidence the extent of planetary urbanization.[14] For example, by 2050 cities in Africa are estimated to grow cumulatively by an additional 950 million people.[15] Urbanization has extended beyond increasingly concentrated megacities to the creation of dispersed urban territories. In this way, the urbanization process is often most vigorous at the edges of or between cities, in sites co-opted by urban processes. These processes are typically driven by economic imperatives, the extension of infrastructure, or political agency. Recent urban discourse has investigated how the extension of urban processes into rural territory has produced landscapes that can no longer be distinguished by the binary distinction between urban and rural. In China, for example, a unique spatial fabric has been created by the unfolding dynamics of rural-urban transformation there. This is the result of a diverse set of factors that include top-down governmental policies and bottom-up entrepreneurial actions of villagers—in some cases the government expropriates village land for large-scale development projects while in others the remittances sent to rural areas by the younger generation working in cities are used to replace traditional mud brick dwellings with concrete—frame, modernized homes. Either way, this leads to villages with increasing building densities yet diminishing populations. In other places, villages are demolished and villagers relocated as a consequence of infrastructural development.[16] This all produces a variety of conditions and gradations in territory that the terms *rural* and *urban* are no longer useful in defining.

The urbanization process is often most vigorous at the edges of or between cities, in sites co-opted by urban processes. These processes are typically driven by economic imperatives, the extension of infrastructure, or political agency.

Rural and urban forms of living have also been brought into question by the COVID-19 pandemic. For both urban and rural dwellers, the pandemic has furthered our interiority, our dependency on the screen, and our reliance on technology. At the same time, the city, as a concentration of people, interaction, and exchange, has become a site of increased risk of infection. The SARS outbreak of 2003 in Hong Kong showed how contagion could spread via shared infrastructural pipes within dense apartment buildings. Having experienced this, the Hong Kong government's response to COVID-19 has been draconian. The government imposed the compulsory testing of buildings and the complete gating and isolation of entire neighborhood blocks in districts such as Yau Ma Tei.[17] Apartments with access to fresh air from balconies and houses with gardens have become even more coveted. This has exposed the increasing polarization of populations in spatial terms, manifesting divisions explicitly and rendering the poorest and most disenfranchised communities the hardest hit.[18]

As a reaction to the pandemic, future populations may witness a shift from increasingly concentrated urban areas to more distributed and sparser settlements. Those with the economic mobility to leave may choose to abandon the city, furthering the stratification of society. This would not be dissimilar to the formation of the original suburbs of the nineteenth century as domestic escapes for the privileged few from the pollution and squalor of the industrial city made possible through railway infrastructure, or the twentieth-century exurbs that resulted from the rise of the car. The question remains as to whether twenty-first-century advances in technological connectivity will lead to as profound a shift in types of settlement. The commuter belt, particularly in areas around global cities like London, supports a lifestyle of working in the city and living in the countryside that has altered rural livelihoods, supplanting agricultural production with more consumption-based economies such as tourism, leisure, and recreation.

The pandemic forced the global workforce into new work-home relationships that sidelined the standard five-day-per-week office model for more flexible systems of work. Whether these will be maintained once the pandemic has dissipated also remains to be seen, yet they are indicative of a potential scenario whereby the need to commute to work may soon be surpassed.

View of Chingeltei-16 ger district looking towards the city center, just 6km (3.7 miles) away.

What the pandemic has made evident is that, unlike the contingent risks associated with highly concentrated urban areas, the rural represents a safe haven, and that highly connected remoteness may become the new idyll.

Yet urbanization has continued unabated during the pandemic. This is because of the growth of developing economies where rural-to-urban migration offers the potential of poverty alleviation through access to higher paying jobs. For example, between 2019 and 2021 the populations of Dhaka and New Delhi increased by 1,457,000 and 1,782,000, respectively.[19] Such growth is often characterized by informal urbanization processes, usually in the form of self-built houses that in many parts of the world are dominated by the generic construction system of a concrete frame structure with brick infill. Effectively, this is the model of Le Corbusier's Maison Dom-Ino from 1914 —the universal housing system that was designed for adaptation in its use and organization of internal spaces. Its proliferation globally is a testament to its affordability, ease of construction, and flexibility. It is such a robust model that it has transcended climate, limitations of craft, cultural specificity, and tradition. However, these very attributes have led to vernacular typologies and building techniques becoming increasingly obsolete as such generic modes of construction supersede the specific vernacular. Furthermore, the concrete-frame and infill model encourages and is predominantly used for private dwellings on individual plots. Collective issues of settlement—infrastructure and sanitation, public space and communal programs, the reduction of sprawl, carbon emissions—are overlooked.

Throughout history the desire to control and upgrade informal urban settlements has led to the relocation of inhabitants, land grabs, exploitation and corruption, and often disenfranchisement. The modernist urban project has been fraught with contradictory imperatives: on the one hand, it hopes to offer an alternative to revolution, as foreseen by Le Corbusier in 1923, by building improved and sanitary homes;[20] on the other hand, it proposes to achieve this through wholesale demolition—and with that, the erasure of established social ties and local economies. Today, in the aftermath of both the perceived and real failures of the modernist project to solve the provision of affordable housing, the onus has shifted away from the welfare state towards other models of development including public-private partnerships, development agencies, global financial institutions, or the private sector alone. Planned urbanization under these models simultaneously reinforces systems of control, including compliance to mortgages and legal tenure and stimulates free-market speculation through the commodification of land and property. Effectively, the mechanisms of the free-market are commandeered to supply and deliver affordable housing. This begs the fundamental question of whether it is possible to realize social objectives within the unrelenting prevalence of the capital markets of land and housing. In the context of upgrading infrastructure and improving housing in developing countries or informal settlements, the task is to ensure that the push towards betterment does not become an excuse for neoliberal development models at the expense of low-income communities.

THE ROLE OF THE ARCHITECT

In recent years, some architects and urban planners have increasingly moved away from calling informal settlements "slums," a demeaning term that also implies the need for their removal and replacement. Instead, they propose to look at informal settlements as sources of grassroots innovation, pragmatic construction solutions, and community-based social ties. Some have argued that these settlements demonstrate a source of urban intelligence from which we can discern and extract methods that can be applied to design projects.[21] Yet often the conclusion of these case studies is an urgent call for "new tools" and alternative methods of engagement without actually offering any tangible design methods to do so. Despite architects' demonstrated interest in researching, documenting, and analysing the phenomena of informal settlements around the world, the role of the architect as an active agent in delivering impactful projects in the urban transformation process seems to have withered since the 1970s. Why have we lost the capacity as professionals to test and invent new typologies of affordable housing for such conditions? Have insecurities from the failure of the modernist project and the hegemony of the market rendered us truly incapacitated?

The lack of agency of the architect in the design and planning of informal settlements and the fundamental issues associated with rural-to-urban transformation has not always been the case. Team X, a group of architects that included Jaap Bakema, Georges Candilis, Giancarlo De Carlo, Aldo van Eyck,

In the context of upgrading infrastructure and improving housing in developing countries or informal settlements, the task is to ensure that the push towards betterment does not become an excuse for neoliberal development models at the expense of low-income communities.

Alison and Peter Smithson, and Shadrach Woods was disillusioned with the dominant discourse of modern architecture as espoused by CIAM under the leadership of Walter Gropius, Siegfried Giedion, and Le Corbusier. The split caused by their disagreement eventually resulted in the dissolution of CIAM in 1959, followed by the first formal meeting of Team X the next year.[22] Team X countered what they saw as the conformity and universality of modern planning and instead argued for the creation of *habitats*. These were defined as urban organisms—intersecting public space, housing, and environment within a dynamic context that could grow and change over time. A new awareness emerged to tackle and engage with the most pressing and escalating processes of urbanization, namely the creation of slums and shanty towns as a result of industrialization at the fringes of cities in locations as diverse as Latin America and Africa. This paradigm shift was exemplified by PREVI (Proyecto experimental de vivienda, or Experimental Housing Project) in Lima, Peru, from 1965 to 1973.[23] Commissioned by the Peruvian government with the United Nations Development Program, British architect Peter Land, who had befriended the Peruvian president Fernando Belaúnde Terry, organized a competition for the design and construction of 1,500 affordable homes on a site eight kilometers north of Lima. Despite the tabularasa site and fixed masterplan, it was an opportunity for Team X members such as Aldo van Eyck, Candilis-Josic-Woods, and associated figures like James Stirling and harles Correa to test low-rise, high-density prototypical housing models that were structured to grow and adapt over time. For example, Stirling's prototype used a prefabricated "climbing frame" that would structure the growth of four dwellings around a central courtyard.[24] The project consisted of a government-funded first phase that provided this support structure, which subsequently residents infilled to meet their housing needs.

Since PREVI, the mechanisms of implementing low-cost housing by international organizations such as the UN have fundamentally changed. In 1976, the first Habitat conference and resultant Vancouver Action Plan called for a need to engage with the deleterious effects of unparalleled urbanization occurring in developing countries at the time. Architects such as John Turner pioneered methods to assist people to take ownership in the construction of their homes,[25] and "sites and services" became the predominant method of implementation by agencies such as the World Bank. Although not intended by Turner, the rhetoric shifted away from the ability of the architect to offer expertise in the design of peoples' homes towards the immediacy of providing basic sanitation, thus lacking the integrated approach of the habitat at the core of the thinking of Team X and projects such as PREVI. In 2002, UN Habitat was formed to promote "transformative change in cities and human settlements." It is an astonishing fact that architects, who were at the core of Habitat's conception, with the involvement of both Buckminster Fuller and Paolo Soleri in 1976, are completely absent from UN Habitat's current board. Indeed, the New Urban Agenda from 2016, called Habitat III, contains no mention of how architects can contribute to urban transformation in its 194-page document.[26]

In parallel, the mechanisms of financing projects have also changed. From the 1970s to today, the role of international institutions such as the World Bank and Asian Development Bank has shifted away from directly funding and implementing projects to providing loan agreements to national governments. And implementation tends to be carried not by the governments but by the private sector. In some cases, the dependency on financial tools such as mortgages leaves gaps in the development process, as the lowest income brackets are often excluded or denied loan agreements. At the same time, reliance on loan rates, which are often high interest, increases the debt burden to some of the most vulnerable in the population. In Mongolia, the promise of low-interest green mortgages supplied by the Green Climate Fund (set up by the United Nations Framework Convention on Climate Change in 2010) has been waylaid by the punitive exchange rate between the US dollar and Mongolia's depreciating local currency, effectively making local banks unwilling to take financial risks.

Clearly, there is a need and an opportunity for architects to reclaim a role in the transformation of urban settlements as a critical issue of our time. When PREVI was built in 1973, 33 million people lived in informal settlements. Today there are more than one billion.[27] The approach of Team X and the prototypes developed for PREVI are invaluable evidence of the innovative capability of architects to develop models of incremental growth and to consider the interconnection between dwellings and the urban realm. Given the reliance on complex financial mechanisms to deliver urban projects, architects should be able to navigate those systems, but they must also look for opportunities and potential loopholes when such systems stagnate and fail.

LEARNING FROM, AND ACTING IN, ULAANBAATAR

This book is conceptualized as a *Learning from ...* model. It uses the example of Ulaanbaatar to understand the processes of urbanization through the lens of architecture. The intent of this investigation is to extract a methodology —what we refer to conceptually as a *framework*—to assert the architect as a key participant in the process of urbanization. As demonstrated in this book, our work in Ulaanbaatar tests how the architect can build a framework that originates from a specific understanding of the context in which people conduct their everyday lives. The ger districts illustrate how a single dwelling type, the ger, can have a massive effect on the development of urban fabric, which prompts us to consider how new typologies could impact and transform the city. If the Maison Dom-Ino type demonstrates how the design of an archetypal dwelling can have a profound impact on the urbanization process, it follows that there is architectural potential to rethink the design of the basic unit of habitation towards other new objectives, including adaptation, public space, and sustainability. If the ger is part of the problem, it can also become part of the solution, by evolving its design in response to new contextual demands of permanence and environmental performance.

This architectural project challenges the notion that the master plan is an effective tool to shape emerging urban conditions and instead advocates for a more agile model of development. Unlike the master plan, the project is based on incrementality and the construction of a network of stakeholders through the process of design and building.

This architectural project challenges the notion that the master plan is an effective tool to shape emerging urban conditions and instead advocates for a more agile model of development. Unlike the master plan, the project is based on incrementality and the construction of a network of stakeholders through the process of design and building. The objective is to instigate typological change that has a positive impact on the process of urban transformation. In our case, such new typologies emerge from prototypes: built experiments that can be evaluated according to their performance and through feedback from residents and other stakeholders such as local government officials, development agencies, and financial institutions. The work of prototyping is therefore an iterative process, in constant dialogue with the context in which it is located.

Our method has been distilled through working in the ger districts over the last seven years. In this time we have been actively involved in a variety of projects, including waste collection infrastructure, community buildings, housing, and urban strategies. In the process, we have encountered dead ends, witnessed the demolition of our built work, and received resistance from residents. The story of our experiences demonstrates the difficulties of working in a context as exacting as Mongolia—where the extremely cold climate, the need for practical construction solutions, and the limited economic resources underpins every design decision. These extreme pragmatics lead to precise definitions of form, building tectonics, and integrations of environmental infrastructure. It is a lived narrative that leads to our proposal for a new development model, in the form of the Incremental Development Manual printed towards the end of this book. The manual contains choices of house types to meet different family incomes and needs, as well as mechanisms to finance them and scenarios of how clusters of families could work together to provide infrastructure and configure shared common ground.

Although specific to the ger districts of Ulaanbaatar, the story of how people, communities, planners, and politicians grapple with the effects of planetary urbanization remains one of the critical issues of the twenty-first century. How this process will be materialized and organized spatially, and by whom, will have profound ramifications for the climate as well as the social and economic makeup of our cities. In responding to these urgent issues, this book affirms the architect's vital contribution to the discourse on the process of *becoming urban,* a position that architects once led.

The story of how people, communities, planners, and politicians grapple with the effects of planetary urbanization remains one of the critical issues of the twenty-first century. How this process will be materialized and organized spatially, and by whom, will have profound ramifications for the climate as well as the social and economic makeup of our cities.

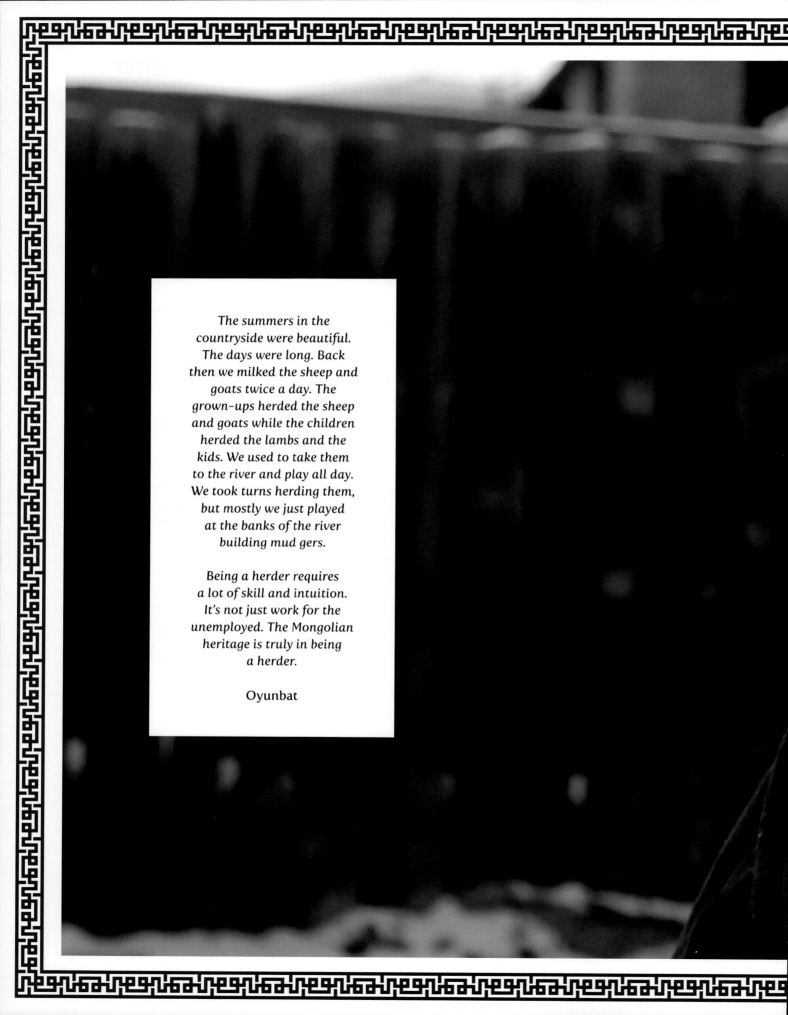

*The summers in the
countryside were beautiful.
The days were long. Back
then we milked the sheep and
goats twice a day. The
grown-ups herded the sheep
and goats while the children
herded the lambs and the
kids. We used to take them
to the river and play all day.
We took turns herding them,
but mostly we just played
at the banks of the river
building mud gers.*

*Being a herder requires
a lot of skill and intuition.
It's not just work for the
unemployed. The Mongolian
heritage is truly in being
a herder.*

Oyunbat

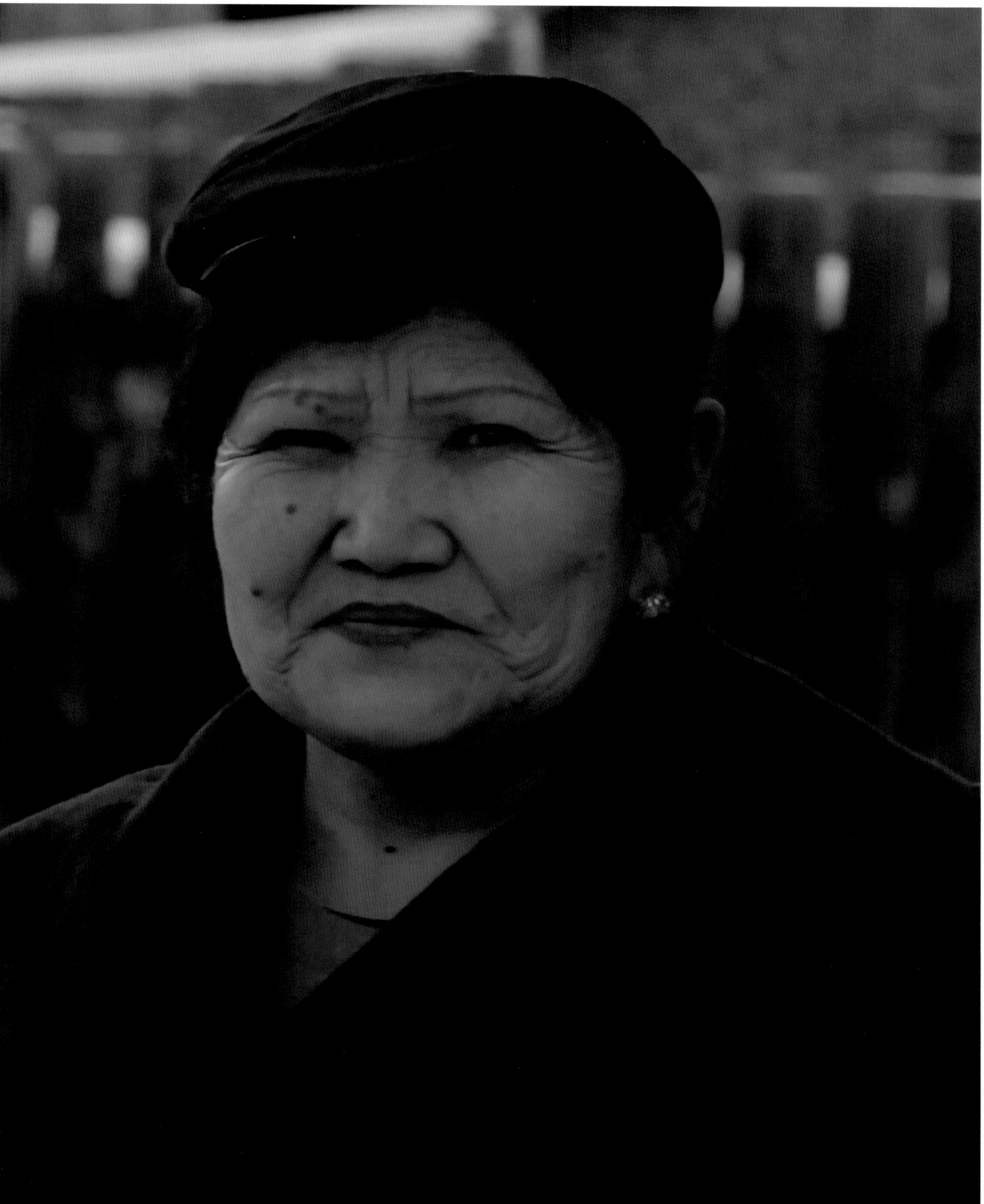

SETT
LING

THE
NOMADS

View of Ulaanbaatar in 1957 showing newly constructed apartment buildings adjacent to a ger area.

SETTLING
THE NOMADS

Today a visit to the ger districts of Ulaanbaatar reveals a context that is a complex interplay between the urban and the rural that has formed its own unique identity and spatial character. It is not an in-between condition on a linear trajectory from nomadic to sedentary life but something distinct, offering a viable alternative between the countryside and the traditional city center.

Ger districts are not new phenomena. They have always been present in Mongolian cities, functioning as sites of exchange and reconciliation between nomadic and urban life. Historically, ger districts would expand and contract at the edges of more permanent settlements in response to seasonal trading or religious festivals. To this day, any permanent urban center in Mongolia still has its own contingent ger district. However, their evolution on the fringes of Ulaanbaatar represents something new. Here the ger districts have become sedimented into an urban fabric, containing over 840,000 residents who mostly own their land and their property.[28] It could be argued that they make up the defining entity of Ulaanbaatar itself. A proportion of ger district residents are migrants who moved only recently from the countryside.[29] For these recent arrivals, the districts do represent a hinge between urban and rural life, a place of transition from nomadic to sedentary living and assimilation to urban life. Other new residents came after giving up on city apartment living, having chosen the ger districts as an affordable opportunity to own land and build a house. At the same time, 45 percent of residents have lived in the ger districts for over 20 years and have no intention of moving.[30]

This group of ger district natives represents an emerging population that calls the districts home. They have a sense of belonging and intend to stay in the ger districts and improve their living situation.

The different generations can be categorized into those who lived through Soviet state control and the upheavals of the transition to a free-market economy and democracy in 1990 and those who never experienced the communist state. Currently, 52.6 percent of the 840,000 ger district residents were born in Ulaanbaatar after 1990. This means that over half of the inhabitants both never experienced communism and never lived as nomads.[31] This group of ger district natives represents an emerging population that calls the districts home. They have a sense of belonging and intend to stay in the ger districts and improve their living situation. This group asserts that the ger districts have become a distinct type, an equal third amongst the city and the countryside.

In order to contextualize the creation of that spatial identity, this chapter describes critical moments of historical change that shaped the territorial transformation of the country in terms of nomadic, urban, and ger district life.

NOMADIC LIFE

It is paradoxical to learn about the city from a culture that is intrinsically non-urban. Indeed, the logics of the pastoral lifestyle in Mongolia are anti-urban. Households are sparsely distributed across a wide territory to avoid the mixing of animals from different herds and preserve local resources and pastures, which means that people typically meet sporadically and in small groups.[32] This is reflected in the lack of a definitive word for community in the Mongolian language.[33] The spatial separation between public and private are therefore fundamentally different for traditional nomads than for sedentary urban cultures. In urban societies, daily life is typically articulated through a spatial hierarchy between what is public and shared and what is private and the domain of the individual or household. In contrast, for Mongolian nomads there is typically only the ger and the open land of the steppe. This means that the ger operates as both the most private and the most public setting. Its single space accommodates a range of activities for the family and is also used to welcome and entertain guests. The land too has this duality: it is both the most collective space, identified as a shared territory for all Mongolians, and can be the most intimate and private. In an interview, friend and collaborator Badamkhand Bayar described how the *uurga*, or herding stake, can be placed into the ground to demarcate and signal the site of a couple's love making. This illustrates that our Western assumptions about public, private, and the spatial hierarchy that architecture helps to shape and organize must be reassessed in order to respond to the uniqueness of Ulaanbaatar's present-day condition.

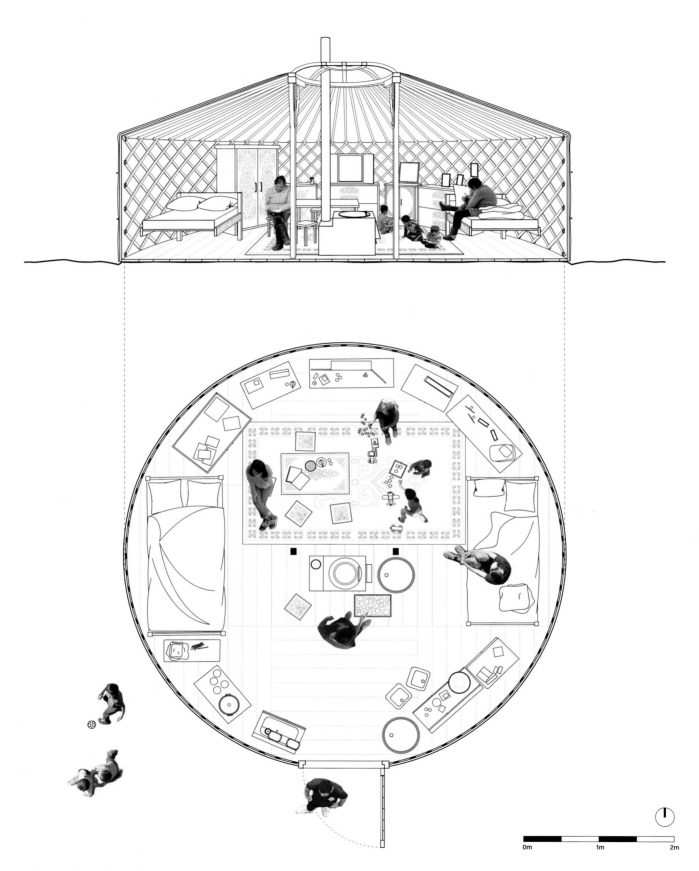

The traditional Mongolian ger.

0m   1m   2m

To further understand the forces that still resonate within the ger districts as well as the ones that have become obsolete, it is helpful to trace the basic spatial and territorial logics of nomadic life across three periods: before Soviet state control (pre-1924); Soviet collectivization (1924–1990); and privatization (1990 onwards). The following brief historical primer aims to untangle what life as a nomad has meant in the context of Mongolia's two most significant paradigm shifts of the last 100 years, which align with two of the most significant ideological transformations that occurred in the twentieth century: communism and free-market capitalism. In the case of Mongolia, the systemic change into the free-market led to a more radical alteration of nomadic societal organization than that of collectivization under communist state control.

TERRITORIAL CONTROL WITHOUT PERMANENCE

The first territorial divisions were undertaken during the Mongol Empire (founded in 1206 by Chinggis Kahn) to consolidate tribes by dividing the empire into territorial fiefdoms.[34] Emerging settlements formed at trading posts along caravan routes or at border trading posts between Russia or China. Often Chinese traders dominated these permanent settlements, with Mongolians occupying ger camps at the periphery. Karakhorum, the capital of the Mongol empire in the thirteenth century, was a key node in this Silk Road network, and included architecture from Chinese and Muslim influences until it was destroyed in 1380 by Ming troops.

From 1586 on, the influence of Buddhism and the creation of monasteries and lamaseries was enmeshed with the fiefdoms of Mongol princes.[35] Monasteries became administrative control points and trading hubs, often located strategically along nomadic pasture routes and in areas with plentiful grassland and sources of water. This was reinforced and strengthened during the Qing Dynasty. The Manchus awarded territory to loyal Mongol princes, who allocated seasonal pasture routes to herders in return for the provision of set amounts of animal products and livestock for the monastery. In this way the monasteries were centers of wealth accumulation and spirituality, but also developed into bases of knowledge and expertise in the form of education, medicine, and astrology.

For nomads, herder families would encamp in groups from two to ten households as part of a *Khot ail*, advantageously working and migrating together to share responsibilities and labor. Although animals would pasture together, ownership, and therefore wealth, was still by each individual family. Membership of the Khot ail would fluctuate, but it would allow poor families to benefit from the shared resources of the group in exchange for labor.[36] Migration patterns would depend on the terrain and climate of the location as well as the speed of the depletion of pastureland, which would occur faster the larger the herd. Typically, the summer months were spent at low elevation, close to a water source in areas of plentiful pasture so hay could be cut and harvested for the winter. Autumn pastures were for fattening the herd in preparation for the winter months, which were spent at higher elevation in mountain ranges providing shelter from the wind. Spring camps would return to lower slopes for birthing and the gradual return to the summer camp.

In the case of Mongolia, the systemic change into the free-market led to a more radical alteration of nomadic societal organization than that of collectivization under communist state control.

This elastic relationship would range from hundreds of miles to single digits and would also vary in number, from a minimum of four moves up to thirty.[37] Though the collapse of the Qing Dynasty in 1911 allowed Mongolia to declare its independence, with Bogd Khaan instated as king and thus religious and political ruler of Mongolia, the formation of the Republic of China in 1912 and the Russian Soviet Republic in 1917 drew Mongolia, sandwiched between these increasingly powerful nations, into a complex set of changing political dynamics. The Chinese nominally reclaimed sovereignty over Mongolia, deposing the monarch, but this was a volatile period of contestation between revolutionary socialist groups and anti-communist warlords. In 1921, Russia provided forces to support Damdin Sukhbaatar, the leader of the Mongolian People's Revolutionary Party, to seize control and establish a new communist state. The incumbent king remained until his death in 1924, signifying the start of a new era of Soviet control.

Mongolia's parliament, ministries, and decision-making processes were all restructured to align with Soviet policy. The Soviet Union retained oversight and provided technological knowledge as well as a military presence that suppressed any uprisings and deterred China from pressing for its own territorial claim.[38]

COLLECTIVIZATION

The communist state destroyed over 700 monasteries and executed 43,000 lamas and religious leaders during the Stalinist purges from 1937 to 1939.[39] After initial efforts to collectivize the herders was met with revolt in 1932, a more gradual process was initiated together with incentives such as tax breaks to encourage herders to join. By 1959 over 99 percent of herders were part of a collective. Rural pastoralism was restructured by creating 300 soums (district centers), which each supported a collective, or negdel, of between 500 and 1000 households. These were further subdivided into brigades of between fifty and one hundred households, and khesegs of twenty. Families would herd animals for the state yet could maintain a maximum of fifty heads per family for their own use.[40] In many cases the soum structure was overlayed onto the same sites as the monasteries, thus the longstanding logics of seasonal migration and sites of trade and exchange were not altered. The sum was the support structure of the collective, containing its administrative center, veterinary services, healthcare, schools with boarding facilities, cultural and social clubs, libraries, and shops.[41] In some cases processing factories were constructed to manufacture sausages, textiles, felt, and other animal biproducts.

Compared to the monastic nomadic patterns, after collectivization the overall distance of migration was reduced, and the construction of winter shelters and wells encouraged routes to become more set and predetermined. To avoid overgrazing, the collective mandated the practice of otor, the deployment of a subgroup of herders to seasonal pastures. This allowed some residents to become more sedentary, staying closer to sum centers. In effect, collectivization organized nomadic practices towards efficiency and increased productivity, enacting the Soviet project of

Diagram of the change in nomadic
herder patterns between pre-Soviet,
Soviet, and free-market periods.

Winter

Winter

Winter

Winter

Spring

Fall

Fall

Fall

Spring

Fall

Spring

Spring

Summer

Summer

Summer

Summer

Monastery
education and trade

Summer

Animal products

Soum

School supports families

Independent
herders

Processing

District

Distribution

Migration to the city

Independent paths organised
by single Monastery

Collective organises migration
and distant 'otor' routes

Unorganised independent
herders lead to territorial conflict

Pre-Revolution	1691-1911
Collectives	1960-1990
Free Market	1990-Now

The countryside in Terelj, a two-hour drive northeast from Ulaanbaatar.

progress through industrialization. In an interview, Tovdoo, a retired ex-nomad currently living in the ger districts, recounted his duties as part of the Malchin Negdel collective in Uvs Province as constant and burdensome. During this period, over one third of Mongolia's GDP was provided by Soviet aid while Soviet-instated procedures and systematic controls became a scaffold for the entire functioning of the country. In this way, the steppe became a highly articulated operational landscape organized through the collective and its mechanisms of hierarchical control.

PRIVATIZATION

The political shift within the USSR towards openness and reform (*glasnost* and *perestroika*) during the 1980s and successive revolutionary waves across Eastern Europe in 1989 resulted in the collapse of the communist block and the eventual disintegration of the USSR in 1991. These events formed the backdrop to Mongolia's own peacefully orchestrated revolution led by Sanjaasürengiin Zorig, which resulted in the resignation of the communist Mongolian People's Party in 1990 and the instatement of a democratic parliament and a free-market economy.[42]

We had obligations to the state, providing milk, curds, and cheese. Every day, we had to bring them to the brigade center, called Zavuud, by horse or by camel. We would just bring the raw products and then they would be processed by others, into butter, cream, and so on. Each household within the khesig *sent their individual member to deliver these products each day. This was a lot of work, we had to milk the livestock once a day, every day. We gave the state all the milk we could give. For us, a family with six to seven hundred animals, our yearly duty was to provide, for example, two to three thousand litres of milk annually, if we didn't meet these obligations we would have to pay ourselves from our private livestock or get salary cuts.*

Tovdoo

The removal of the Soviet armature from the Mongolian economy resulted in real wages falling by 50 percent from 1990 to 1992. Between 1989 and 1994 poverty escalated from 0 to 27 percent of the population. Meanwhile, inflation reached triple digits from 1991 to 1993. In 1991, the state farms and collectives were disbanded and herders offered compensation of ₮10,000 (tugriks, MNT) to purchase their animals to start private herding operations. This increased the number of herders from 135,420 in 1989 to 407,030 by 2001. However, without the state support or the control of the negdel, herding reverted back to a more basic subsistence form.[43]

The benefits of the negdels, including guaranteed income, replenishment of stocks, provision of winter fodder, transportation infrastructure, access to machinery, and the collective operation and coordination of households with shared responsibilities, disappeared. The collapse of state-controlled businesses that supported the agrarian economy within the sum centers resulted in unemployment and a lack of manufacturing capacity that would lead to its inevitable outsourcing. The lack of investment in these townships also meant that essential support structures such as schools, health centers, animal hospitals, and connections to markets could no longer function, so those negdel professionals had little choice but to move to the city.[44]

Those who stayed became herders, often preferring to remain close to their existing homes in the former sum centers. The lack of enforced and coordinated seasonal migration, which had often been assisted by collectivized transportation, led to a more sedentary form of herding. Without movement, pastures were overgrazed, and disputes over trespassing increased. To protect their territory, herders would move even less, compounding the issue of deteriorating grassland.

The extreme winters, or *dzuds,* between 1999 and 2001, led to over 11 million animals dying.[45] This exposed the vulnerabilities of the herders without the support of the collective to provide winter fodder—in some instances even by helicoptering in hay—or to assist in restocking the herd.

Without a herd or the means to start again with a new one, and without the possibility of employment in sum centers, affected herders faced no alternative other than to move to the city. That city was the capital, Ulaanbaatar.

During a dzud, everything becomes blindingly white. ... The sky and ground all melt into one monotonous white sheet. ... Ripples of snow wash over the ground all the time. In the winter, livestock use their hooves to dig through the snow for grass. When the snow is rock hard, they can't do that anymore. The animals' hooves start cracking and they start limping. Then there's nothing they can do except lay on the ground and you feed them on the ground.... Eventually, they just die ...

Oyunbat

PARADIGM SHIFT

With the dismantling of the economic and organizational scaffold of Soviet-supported collectivization, nomadic life has become increasingly challenging for many herders. Supporting industries of animal byproducts and processing within Mongolia have also collapsed due to lack of investment and technological progression. The emergence of China's industrial capacity to process goods incredibly cheaply meant that it superseded Mongolia's national manufacturing ability, leaving Mongolia primarily a producer of raw materials. Today the resource sector is responsible for almost 90 percent of Mongolia's total exports, and 90 percent of those raw materials go to China.[46]

The Soviet state apparatus may have been artificial, in the sense that it was propping up industrial production, but it provided an effective structure that linked pastoralism with a larger network of industrial townships. The shift into the free-market economy decoupled those dependencies and exposed the weaknesses of the existing industrial infrastructure. Soviet aid amounted to one third of Mongolia's GDP, and nearly 30 percent was directed into supporting rural townships and the rural economy. While foreign aid to Mongolia from Japan, Western nations, and international finance institutions amounted to 25 percent of GDP by 1996, this money was often used to countenance the vulnerabilities of the financial sector, with the IMF having provided debt bailouts six times since 1990.[47]

The prolonged de-investment in the rural since 1990 coincided with a land law in 2002 that granted every Mongolian citizen the right to claim and legally own a plot of land of 700 square meters. Before this law was introduced, the population of Ulaanbaatar had grown by 256,000 from 1990 to 2002. Since the law, however, the population has doubled, growing from a total of 828,000 in 2002 to 1.6 million in 2020,[48] demonstrating the attractiveness of being able to own land in the capital. Today, Ulaanbaatar houses almost 50 percent of the country's entire population of 3.3 million.

The significance of such figures is to demonstrate that the paradigm shift from Soviet state control to the free-market represented a change in the organization of the entire country in spatial terms. During collectivization, the Soviets overlayed their model of organization onto the underlying patterns of nomadic pastoral life, maintaining existing seasonal migration routes while imposing systematic controls and building up the rural economy through differentiation of labor and manufacturing industries. That is to say, there was continuity, albeit within a completely different ideological setup. Without that administrative structure after 1990, the fragmentation of the collectives into private herding groups and the depletion of financial resources to support the pastoral economy inevitably led to economic hardship for many herders and township workers, with limited options other than to move to the capital. The dual push and pull created in just three years from 1999 to 2002—the push by the extreme weather of the dzuds that wiped out many animals and the pull of opportunities to own land in the city—drove many more to move from the countryside to the capital city. As a result, since the 1990 democratic revolution, the urban population has tripled, and the city's administrative territory has expanded to over thirty times its original size.[49]

If these two critical stages of transformation during the Soviet and free-market era had significant consequences for nomadic life in terms of its operation and territorial occupation, then how was urban life impacted? How did the city change during the socialist period and how has the post-revolution city been redefined and transformed by different models of economic and urban development?

As a result, since the 1990 democratic revolution, the urban population has tripled, and the city's administrative territory has expanded to over 30 times its original size.

Back then the Russians built many residential complexes and awarded apartments to those who worked hard. We were awarded our apartment then and lived there from 1986 to 2002. When we lived in apartments, we all had jobs. Everything was convenient and comfortable. We had running hot water. Our kids all went to school and everything was organized and followed a program. It was comfortable. We didn't have to worry about heating the home or getting cold or anything like that.

Erdenechimeg Ishjamts

The Gandan district today.

URBAN
LIFE

The first settlement of Ulaanbaatar, Urguu, was founded in 1639 by Mongol nobles to consolidate Mongolian national interests as a reaction to the occupation of Inner Mongolia by the Manchus. Operating as a monastic trading post, the town itself was nomadic for its first 139 years, relocating somewhere between twenty-five and forty times before occupying the area of the current city.[50] Mongolia succumbed to the Qing Dynasty in 1691, and it was this influence, together with the influx of traders and religious figures, which resulted in the formation and growth of more permanent structures in the area.

These eventually developed into the settlement of Ikh Khuree, which was administrated from 1778 to implement Qing policies. During this period, the city evolved into a religious and trade node where Buddhism and commerce thrived. This initiated the creation of more permanent structures within the emerging city. Accounts of the settlement at this time describe a mixture of permanent brick and stone structures mainly associated with religious buildings, some residents living in low-rise mud huts, and expanding areas of ger districts housing traders and monks alike.[51] Traces of this embryonic city remain: the temple structures built between 1834 and 1838 within the Gandantegchlin monastery led to the formation of a ger district around its edges that forms the Gandan area today, the territory inscribed by the district having outlasted the impermanent nature of its building typology.

IMPOSED URBAN ORDER

The establishment of the Mongolian socialist state in 1921 marked the beginning of a new sedentarization era across the country. Although Mongolia was never incorporated into the Soviet Union, the USSR maintained political control by embedding loyal leaders in the government. They were empowered to deliver on Soviet policy directives and to swiftly suppress any voices of dissent. Those who did not comply were sent to Moscow for reeducation, with some never returning.[52]

Because the communist project itself evolved from the urban inequalities associated with industrialization, its ideology was intrinsically urban, so the Soviets pressed for the construction of a new industrialized urban society, which they supported through trade and economic agreements, finance, and by providing technical expertise. Decision-making within the parliament and across bureaus was restructured to implement these directives. The territory was subdivided into a hierarchical structure of administrative units to deliver the Soviet plans, ranging from the Kheseg (neighborhood) to *Khoroo* (sub-district) to *Düüreg* (district), while the number of *Aimags* (provinces) was increased from five to eightteen. In effect, the mechanism to realize the socialist project was seen to be urbanization, and as the nation's capital, Ulaanbaatar became the focus of this drive.

Ulaanbaatar was established in 1924 as a bounded administrative entity with Soviet funding for infrastructure and urban development modelled on Soviet plans, building typologies, and social organization. Effectively, this Soviet urbanization project imposed a conceptually alien order of fixed urban systems, including transportation networks, apartment blocks, factories, and social and educational institutions. It also involved the erasure of most of the only permanent historical structures, the monasteries. City building commenced in the 1920s by using imported Soviet designs and prefabricated concrete technology to build U-shaped, C-shaped, and linear-slab apartment blocks that flanked the main east–west thoroughfare of Peace Avenue. Additionally, civic infrastructure in the form of the parliament building (1926), the central library (1921), and Sukhbaatar Square (1937–50) were established to reflect the new urban order of the Soviet city. Captured Japanese prisoners of war from the battle of Khalkhin Gol in 1939 were press-ganged to construct some of these buildings, including the Opera House (1943) and Stock Exchange building (1945).[53]

Urban plans were stalled because of World War II. The Giprogor Institute in Moscow developed the first postwar master plan for the city in 1954, and subsequently went on to develop additional masterplans in 1961, 1975, and 1986.[54] The first plan established the overall structure of the city: the road layout; a central district for government, universities, and banks; residential districts complete with water, sewage, electricity, and heating infrastructure; and a separate industrial zone that initially focused on animal byproducts including shoes, leather, soap, textiles, clothing, and felt. The plan predicted the population would reach 120,000 by 1974, but by 1960 the population had already reached 180,000.[55] This pattern continued through successive master plans that tried to keep pace with

In effect, the mechanism to realize the socialist project was seen to be urbanization, and as the nation's capital, Ulaanbaatar became the focus of this drive.

the growth of the city yet continually underestimated population rates.[56] As a result, as each new construction phase replaced ger settlements with permanent housing, new ger districts continued to extend out from the city's northern fringes to accommodate new arrivals.

Industry was also developed during the 1960s and 1970s, with new zones created to support mechanics, construction materials, timber yards, breweries, and meat packing. The final iteration of the master plan in 1986 sought to limit the expanse of the city, develop satellite towns, and remove residual and obsolete programs from central areas. But the plan was never realized due to the 1990 democratic revolution. The subsequent period of economic restructuring followed the neoliberal model advocated by international financial organizations like the International Monetary Fund (IMF) and the World Bank.

These new economic forces have begun to alter the city, inserting new building typologies and commercial development projects. However, the main underlying spatial and organizational structure of the city remains a legacy of the Soviet-supported urban development project between 1921 and 1990.

RESHAPING THE SOVIET CITY
In the wake of the revolution, socialist iconography was not systematically erased as in other post-Soviet countries, but in Ulaanbaatar some socialist symbols and statues were removed, and some streets were renamed. However, both Buddhism and Chinggis Kahn, which were prohibited during the Soviet era, have made a resurgence as sources of post-revolution Mongolian national identity.[57] In the capital, this reidentification with Chinggis Khan has been expressed in the renovation of the Mongolian parliamentary buildings (2005–06) that replaced the mausoleum of socialist leaders Sukhbaatar and Choibalsan with a statue of Chinggis Khan and other key figures from the period of the great Mongol Empire (1206–1368).[58]

However, the main force that has reshaped the Soviet city since 1990 has been the impact of free-market economic development. This is pronounced near the monumental Sukhbaatar Square as it meets Peace Avenue. Development models involving international finance and local conglomerates have resulted in the construction of towers that include the seventeen-story, glass-fronted Central Tower (2009), which contains luxury brands such as Louis Vuitton and telecommunications company Unitel, the iconic curving-arch profile of the Blue Sky Hotel (2009), and just behind that the ICC Tower (2009) that headquarters Xac Bank and the Italian Embassy.

The main force that has reshaped the Soviet city since 1990 has been the impact of free-market economic development.

The lack of clear planning controls in the aftermath of the 1990 revolution led to opportunistic land grabs also led to opportunistic land grabs, particularly on public spaces or residual land. Inadequate survey information with clear allocation of ownership has made it easier for land to be carved out from public spaces and used for private development. In the courtyards of the Soviet residential U-blocks, for example, the public spaces intended for children's playgrounds or gardens have been infringed on by commercial development. In another example, it has been stated that two nightclubs and three company offices were built on the grounds of the Mongolian National University.[59]

More recently, in 2015, the completion of the Shangri-La complex represents the introduction into Ulaanbaatar of a lifestyle enclave, containing a hotel, shopping mall, restaurants, and high-end residential and office space. The project was co-funded by the Hong Kong–based tycoon Robert Kuok's Shangri-La Group and the Mongolian conglomerate MCS. The MCS group's history is demonstrative of the neoliberalisation of the economy since 1990. Starting as an expert consultancy in 1993 conducting energy projects for international development agencies, in the late nineties MCS expanded into importing commodities, before buying up other companies and assets to diversify its holdings into mining, alcohol, soft drinks, real estate, cashmere, and telecommunications. Today, it has offloaded some assets and business and restructured with ventures into new sectors that include engineering, energy, communications, consumer goods, and healthcare, while retaining its mining interests.

EXTRACTIVE ECONOMIES

The impact of mining has had a profound effect on the Mongolian economy. Despite at times propelling double-digit growth (topping 17 percent of GDP in 2011), the industry's dominance has created volatile conditions of boom-and-bust cycles that have led to debt dependency. The increased reliance on mining of the entire nation's economic forecast has underpinned many of the commercial developments in the city, but it has also led to the inability of the city and the country to move forward with more stable forms of urban development.

The fragility of the economy and its dependency on mining as collateral for further borrowing inevitably leads to increased debt. This boom-bust-bailout cycle erodes investor confidence, deepens the country's debt dependency, and makes long-term strategic planning difficult due to a lack of stable revenue streams.

Mongolia has rich deposits of mineral resources, estimated at the twelfth largest copper reserves and the fourth largest coal reserves in the world. Only one third of its territory has yet to be fully explored. This has attracted huge injections of direct foreign investment, contributing 40 percent of the country's GDP in 2011.[60] However, the capriciousness of commodity markets and a drop in prices between 2014 and 2016 reduced the GDP contribution to just 2 percent. This led to an urgent financial injection of three billion dollars in 2017 from the Bank of Mongolia, which was tied to a sixth bailout package from the IMF to prop up the nation's economy. The fragility of the economy and its dependency on mining as collateral for further borrowing inevitably leads to increased debt. This boom-bust-bailout cycle erodes investor confidence, deepens the country's debt dependency, and makes long-term strategic planning difficult due to a lack of stable revenue streams.

One case in particular, the ongoing narrative regarding the Oyu Tolgoi copper and gold mine that was discovered in 2009, reflects an ongoing debate and a series of paradoxes regarding Mongolia's mineral wealth. Such natural resources could salvage the country's economic woes yet require huge amounts of investment in infrastructure for extraction. Although Mongolia is keen to preserve its national rights to its resources, it lacks available finances to fund this development and so is reliant on outside investments from global corporations such as Rio Tinto to help fund and operate extraction processes. Under the 2009 investment agreement for Oyu Tolgoi, Rio Tinto owns 51 percent of Turquoise Hill Resources, which in turn owns 66 percent of the mine, with the Mongolian government owning the remaining 34 percent. As part of that deal, it was identified that the supply of domestic power was essential to ensure the mine's profitability and to proceed with the development of underground expansion. Currently, power is supplied at a cost of $150–200 million per year from China, which is the main purchaser of the copper concentrate solution produced at the mine, amounting to $797.3 million annually.[61] As Mongolia also has the world's largest undeveloped coal mine at Tavan Tolgoi, one of the conditions of the agreement was to build a power plant, at an estimated cost of $500–600 million, to supply domestic energy to Oyu Tolgoi, rather than importing electricity from China. This has not yet been achieved, and the timeframe to do so has been extended to 2023.

The situation leaves Mongolia in an illogical commodity trap: it is exporting coal to China that is being used in China's power plants to import power back at a premium price to be used to extract copper that is then exported back to China, ultimately lessening Mongolia's capacity to profit from its own mineral wealth. Moreover, the cost of developing the underground mine has increased from an estimated $5.3 billion in 2016 to $6.75 billion, with blame purported to be due either to geological reasons, according to Rio Tinto in 2019, or to Rio Tinto's mismanagement, according to a 2021 independent report.[62]

Mining will inevitably remain a core component of Mongolia's economy. Given that copper is an essential component in the technology of electric vehicles and for renewable power, it will be in high global demand as countries aim to transition out of fossil fuels. However, despite collecting $9.3 billion in revenue from mining, oil, and gas between 2006 and 2016, the government is currently having to borrow in order to refinance its debt, raising $600 million in sovereign bonds in 2020 that will have to be paid back with 5.1 percent interest.[63] This produces an extractive economy, leaving Mongolia arguably at a net loss and unable to take control of its abundant natural wealth.

EXTRACTIVE URBANISM

The impact that the mining sector has had on the physical urban transformation of Ulaanbaatar since 1991 has been in the creation of support infrastructure, both in the form of commercial office space for headquarters or subsidiary service industries and in secondary sectors such as hotels, shopping malls, and restaurants. Financial optimism and anticipated injections of capital fuelled a property boom that has added 3.8 million square meters of living space to the city since 2010.[64] This was propelled by the introduction in 2013 of a low-interest mortgage rate of 8 percent for houses up to 80 square meters, backed by money borrowed through the Chinggis Bond, which led to an uptake of mortgages by an average of 44.9 percent each year. Although designed to bolster the affordable housing sector, it has led to an oversupply in the luxury sector.[65]

The reimaging of Ulaanbaatar, from a Soviet city to an investment capital replete with commercial towers and luxury real estate, fuelled the desire for many to leave the countryside and move to the city. However, this built artifice obfuscates the underlying financial obstacles at the core of Mongolia's progress since 1991. The transition to the free-market and the dependency on the extraction economy has been, and remains, volatile.

The privatization of the herds, dissolution of the collectives, and removal of state support structures, coupled with extreme winters, caused many nomads to leave the countryside and move to Ulaanbaatar. The optimism of economic boom periods propelled by mining discoveries furthered the draw of the city, and people moved in escalating numbers, settling at the city's edge in the ever-expanding ger districts. But the lack of stable funds and increasing national debt means that the necessary infrastructural development to service the ger districts is simply unattainable, especially given their constant year on year expansion. For some the shift to a free-market economy has created huge financial rewards, while for others, particularly those residing in the ger districts, the promised wealth from mining has yet to transform their everyday situations. Some, like resident Erdenechimeg Ishjamts, see the country as worse off today than in the Soviet period:

> My name is Erdenechimeg Ishjamts. I'm sixty years old. I'm an Ulaanbaatar resident. My parents are from Undurkhangai soum in Uvs province. I finished high school in Uvs and came to Ulaanbaatar. I attended the Trade and Commerce Polytechnic College. We got married in 1979 and lived in Building 9 in Khoroolol 1. We got an apartment from the Industry Committee of Shoes and Footwear. Back then the Russians built many residential complexes and awarded apartments to those who worked hard. We were awarded our apartment and lived there from 1986 to 2002. Then we fell on hard times and sold the apartment. Most of the people who were awarded apartments back then did the same. They sold their apartments and moved to the ger districts. Since 2002, we've been living in the ger district.

> Everyone worked towards building Mongolia. This was the seventies and eighties. Up until 1992, everyone had jobs and communities. No one had time to idle around. Then in 1992, that ended. This huge system of supply and manufacturing that covered Ulaanbaatar as well 18 aimags disappeared within two years. All the workers became unemployed, and the factories went to just a handful of people when it became private. 3,000 or 4,000 workers went jobless. The free-market system started all wrong. The transition was handled poorly. We're only 3 million people, and if we had all of the factories and everything now, we would have been like a bear. Our old president Ochirbat said he'd make our country a bear. Now it's more like a bar ...[66]

For some the shift to a free-market economy has created huge financial rewards, while for others, particularly those residing in the ger districts, the promised wealth from mining has yet to transform their everyday situations.

The view from Zaisan monument in 2014 shows incomplete real estate development, built during the boom years following the discovery of mineral resources.

My wife is a kindergarten teacher, but she's currently at home looking after our baby son. Because I live in a ger, the first thing I do in the morning is build a fire. Then I prepare the wood and coal for the rest of the day and drop my daughter off at school before heading to work. I spend most of the day working in my studio.

At the moment, I'm focusing on building a house on my plot rather than trying to get an apartment. But the conditions are difficult, like the water for example. To build a house, you have to manually bring the water from the well. Even after you build your house there's still the problem of heating.

Baasansuren Alexander

The expanse of ger districts that carpet the hillsides and valleys of Ulaanbaatar.

GER
DISTRICT
LIFE

Zulaa, twenty-six, and Urangua, thirty-three,[67] live in a ger on the edge of Bayankhoshuu, one of Ulaanbaatar's ger districts, a thirty-minute drive from the city center. Like other migrants to the city they have had to transition to sedentary living. They now have neighbors, take buses and taxis for transportation, and are confronted with debilitating air and ground pollution found in the city. Zulaa works at a printing company where she makes wholesale cardboard boxes and Urangua works at the Gobi Cashmere factory. Their combined monthly income, after taxes, is around ₮1,200,000, or $490.

Due to the lack of basic infrastructure in the ger districts, the couple spends a significant amount of their income, and their time, on basic needs. There is no piped, running water in the district, so they collect and pay for it from the local water kiosk—a round trip of forty minutes that involves lugging plastic containers of water uphill on a trolley—at least eight times per week, rain or shine. There is no sewage infrastructure, so they dug a two-meter-deep pit latrine. When it is full, they will dig another hole. In the extreme winter, with temperatures reaching -40°C (-40°F), the couple must light a coal fire at least three times a day, equating to a fuel cost of 20 to 30 percent of their income.

The couple is far from unique among the 840,000-plus people who live in the ger districts, accounting for over 60 percent of the city's population.[68] With the population of the city growing by an average of 38,000 each year between 2000 and 2019,[69] and 21,000 of those accountable to the ger districts, the urban risks associated with this form of settlement are becoming increasingly threatening, particularly with respect to sanitation, freshwater supply, and air quality. The untreated wastewater from the ger districts contributes to soil pollution, with 88 percent of the total inhabited area of the capital having microbiological contamination exceeding standard levels.[70] And with homes in the ger districts burning through 1 million tons of coal per year, they are also a factor of the toxic air pollution in the city.[71] The consumption of fossil fuels in the ger districts—an average of 3.8–5 tons of unrefined coal per household—is a major contributor to air pollution in the city. In December 2020 average PM2.5 levels in Ulaanbaatar reached 217 mg/m³, which is 8.7 times higher than the World Health Organization's (WHO) recommended daily average.[72] UNICEF and the WHO have reported that children living in the city have 40 percent lower lung function than children living in rural areas.[73] This demonstrates that the current form of settlement in the ger districts has ramifications beyond that of the immediate household and impacts the entire city.

Without the means or capacity of the government to provide infrastructure to the ger districts, these environmental hazards are escalating every year.

Without the means or capacity of the government to provide infrastructure to the ger districts, these environmental hazards are escalating every year. Given the extreme, unrelenting, and compounding issues associated with this form of urban growth, what can be done from the position of the architect-urbanist? Can alternative approaches offer the capacity for large-scale impact? In order to inform any such strategic approach it is neccessary to understand the underpinning logics of the spatial development of the ger districts. To that end, our research explores the unique characteristics of the districts, the process of their transformation, the impact of this form of urbanization on residents, and the reasons why large-scale master plans are difficult to implement.

TRANSFORMATION
The ger districts of Ulaanbaatar sprawl north to the outer reaches of the city: a carpet of urban fabric that climbs up hillsides and oozes into valleys. Formally, the settlement is made up of gers and one-to-two-story brick homes. Fences surround these dwellings demarcating rectangular plots that form a loose, gridded patchwork. It is a visually arresting sight: the nomadic structure of the ger stationary and captured within an enclosure, multiplied endlessly across the undulating surface of the landscape.

Plots on flat land, next to roads, or close to bus stops or water kiosks are the most sought after due to their convenience and relative ease of settling. Although by law each citizen is allocated an available plot through the city's registration system, often new migrants stake their claim to a piece of land simply by demarcating it with wooden fence. Over time this fence line may be extended opportunistically to incorporate a garden or a parking space, or consolidated to form a straighter boundary with a neighbor or to accommodate a road.

Roads begin as dirt accessways between plots, with often multiple tracks traced into the ground at the earliest stage of settlement. Over the course of a year, the preferred, most convenient path is ingrained into the earth and becomes the main road to which subsequent plots organize and align. These roads also organize services in the district, containing water kiosks and sporadically located small shops.

The twice-daily collection of water from water kiosks in Sukhbaatar-16 district.

New migrants claim a plot of land, fence it in, erect their ger, and dig a pit latrine. Over time, if they can afford to, they will build a baishin, or small house, like this family on the edge of Khan-Uul ger district.

The layers of expansion of Songino Khairkhan-43 district from 2005–19 analyzed by comparing historical Google Earth data with a drone survey.

2005   2012   2019

Due to the speed and extent of the growth, infrastructure is retroactively added to the districts based on demand. Bus stops are added as the settlement continues outwards. Water kiosks are implemented to meet the needs of the increasing population. Electricity cables stretch haphazardly on overhead lines between plots, often with multiple families sharing the same source.

This incremental development is also present within the homes. Many families start by adapting their ger to its new fixed location: some add wooden thresholds to the entrance to block the wind, and others add a permanent concrete foundation under the ger to lessen the cold and prevent water damage. Over time, as the family accrues more income, they might start building a small house, or *baishin,* in stages each summer, starting with the foundation, then walls, then roof. Although many families claim the reason for building a house is to have more room divisions, of the nineteen houses we have surveyed, twelve of them did not have wall separations, remaining as singular open spaces that share all the activities of the household—in other words, retaining the same basic organization of the ger.

In terms of administration, each district, or Khoroo, has a leader or representative who is elected and is based in a district office, which also contains offices for land registration, tax, and social services. Each Khoroo contains around 2,000 households and is partitioned into smaller neighborhoods, or Kheseg, representing 250 to 300 households. Kheseg leaders are employed by the Khoroo office and are the communication channel between smaller clusters of residents and local governance. As the population of each Khoroo rises, it can be divided and a new Khoroo created to manage additional needs. For example, in 2019 Songino Khairkhan-31 was split to create Songino Khairkhan-43.

The layers of growth over time are visible in the built fabric of the districts. The predominant narrative is that there are three basic conditions of ger districts based on their distance from the city center: central ger districts are the oldest settlements with smaller plot sizes and higher numbers of apartments and detached houses; mid-districts contain mainly detached houses; and fringe areas are the newest settlements with land still being claimed.[74] However, our research suggests that within each district those typologies exist together, representing different speeds of transformation that are occurring simultaneously.

By drawing the transformation of one sample ger district, Chingeltei-16, from 2009 to 2017 and comparing Google Earth imagery with our own drone footage, we were able to investigate patterns of growth in the urban fabric. Chingeltei-16 contains patches that are densifying, with plots subdividing to an average of 480 square meters (5166.7 foot), while residual sites are infilled, houses predominate, and the streetscape is clearly defined. Chingeltei-16 is also expanding, with a periphery of haphazard fence lines, an average plot size of 748 square meters (8051.4 foot), and an unresolved street pattern containing dead ends and awkward constrictions. This demonstrates that Chingeltei-16 contains different patches that are evolving constantly and transforming at different speeds.

Acrid smoke produced by coal-burning stoves in the ger districts of Zuun Ail, November 2013.

Otgoo and her three children in her ger in Songino Khairkhan-43 district, November 2018.

Densification and consolidation occurs in proximity to new settlers encroaching onto new plots—it is not simply related to distance from the city center. We also discovered that residents do not replace their ger with a house but rather maintain both. In Chingeltei-16 between 2009 and 2017, both the number of gers and the number of houses increased, by 108 percent and 126 percent respectively. This shows that the ger is still integral to residents' lives, as a kitchen, kids' room, spare lodging for guests or visiting family members, a rental unit, or for storage. It is still the cheapest and most flexible form of space-making in the city and the basic unit of habitation for new migrants.

> *We want to build a house; it is every couple's dream.*
>
> Sanchir Batbold

FAMILY CLUSTERS

As part of our design research concerning new dwelling types to promote a more sustainable trajectory for the ger districts, we interviewed and surveyed 12 households in Songino Khairkhan-43 district, 5.5 kilometers northwest of the city center, an area that has grown in population by 51.6 percent since 2000 and currently has over 6,400 migrants settling each year.[75] We wanted to understand the motivations of those residents who do build houses as well as how an individual family plot changes over time. Sanchir Batbold (twenty-six), a trained journalist, lives with her husband Batbaatar (thirty-three), a primary school teacher, and their two children. They live in a ger, heat their home using a stove, and drive to fetch water three times per week from the water kiosk that is ten minutes away. Together they have a combined income of $234 per month. Sanchir was born in the countryside in 1994, four years after Mongolia's democratic revolution and the privatization of herd ownership. As she approached school age at six, her parents decided to sell their herd and move to the city, buying a plot of land. She met her husband in 2010, had their first child in 2013, and decided to move to a plot owned originally by Batbaatar's parents. Batbaatar's mother and his two sisters live next door. Sanchir and Batbaatar have positioned their ger with the same local intelligence as if they were nomads: door oriented north–south to avoid the cold gusts from the north; away from water gulleys and surface runoff; the foundation slightly cut into the hillside to act as a buffer from the wind. Nevertheless, they represent a generation of ger district dwellers that never were nomads and organize their lives without links to the countryside, either as a source income or in terms of family ties, as their close relatives also live in the city.

Sanchir has three neighbors north of her plot. They all share responsibilities such as grocery shopping, collecting water, and childcare. Even though fences separate the plots, there are gaps that allow movement between, enabling the kids to play and to use a small basketball court made by thirty-two-year-old Idersaikhan in the northernmost plot. Each of neighboring plots are in different states of change. Idersaikhan has built a foundation for a baishin but does not yet have enough money to complete the build and so lives with his five family members in a ger, with his mother in a ger next to it. This is also the case for Munkhdalai in the plot below, who has built up the four walls of a baishin but is waiting for the summer to be able to build the roof, so lives with seven family members in a single ger. This seven-person occupancy represents a density of 3.7 square meters (39.8 square foot) per person, denser than the infamous subdivided apartments in Hong Kong, which have a reported density of 5.8 square meters (62,4 square foot) per person.[76] Gunbat, in the western plot, is the most well off, as he has been working in South Korea since 2018 and his wife Oyunsuren works in a bakery. They have two children and constructed their house in 2018.

Despite differences in income and family structure, none of the residents of these four plots have showers or baths, and all of them rely on external pit latrines. Our analysis of the transformation of the four plots demonstrates the incremental and piecemeal process of consolidation towards a more organized strip development along the road. The current plots were scanned using LiDAR (Light Detection and Ranging) to reveal exact topographic information and evidence of land use. The LiDAR data shows that plots with houses have had to cut and level the ground —sometimes removing an estimated 2.5 tons of earth—leaving residual spaces of unusable and unstable slopes. The land that is not built on is used for a variety of uses including material storage, parking, and planting. In some cases, and bathtubs and fridges are brought out from the ger, particularly during the summer. However, most of the land, between 64 percent and 74 percent, has no apparent use indicating the capacity of the plots to densify and gain new programs.

A NEW TYPOLOGY OF INFORMAL SETTLEMENT
At first sight, the repetitive nature of the gers and houses and the way the settlement envelops the topography evokes images of the favelas of São Paolo or Rio de Janeiro. The formation of the ger districts, premised on the migration of nomadic herders moving to the city in search of a better life, also seems to share a familiar story of rural to urban migration. Both factors, the image of the districts and their origins, allude to defining the ger districts as an informal settlement. However, the ger districts are a unique condition. Although they share many commonalities of informal settlements, the majority of residents have legal tenure of both their land and their property. Compare this with the favela of Paraisópolis in São Paolo, an example of an illegal settlement with no security of tenure, or Baishizhou, an urban village in Shenzhen, China, that can be argued to be a form of illegal development but with legal land tenure. Informal settlements typically conform to the United Nations' definition of slums as areas where 50 percent or more of households suffer one or more of the following five indicators: lack of access to clean water, lack of access to sanitation, non-durable housing, insufficient living area, and insecurity of tenure.[77]

Urban villages in China represent a unique typology that has emerged as a consequence of differing land development rights for rural citizens. There, rural land encapsulated by urban-designated development has been developed by rural citizens into housing for migrant workers. Although the land is legally owned and can be developed by rural citizens, the height and total floor area usually surpass regulations. A unique phenomenon of such urban villages in China is that they act as transition points from the rural to the urban, providing low-cost housing, jobs, and community networks for new migrants entering the city. Despite this, their status is threatened as they are seen by planners as aberrations standing in the way of modernizing urban development.[78]

Each winter, an average household consumes four tons of coal, usually bought from roadside vendors like this one photographed in February 2016.

The ger districts have a degree of autonomy relative to the city and the countryside, and thus a different role within the city.

Compared to the Chinese example of rural-to-urban migration, the relationships between the settlement and the city and between the city and the countryside are also very different in Ulaanbaatar. In China, village and city can be argued to be mutually dependent, with migrants providing a vital workforce in cities and at the same time sending monetary remittances back to villages. In comparison, the ger districts have a degree of autonomy relative to the city and the countryside, and thus a different role within the city. In interviews we conducted with ger district residents in 2016,[79] we learned that very few sent money back to the countryside unless it was for payment for dairy or meat products they had received. Sometimes money would be sent in the other direction to pay for car parts, clothing, or animal medicines. The majority visited the countryside only once or twice a year for holidays or to visit relatives. Some respondents with immediate family involved in herding would visit during springtime to assist with livestock offspring and cashmere combing. Most perceived the countryside to have a better standard of living than the city, for instance, in terms of air quality and an easier lifestyle without the pressures and stresses of city life. However, many were drawn to the city by better educational opportunities for their children and healthcare. The residents we interviewed visited the city center only once or twice a week, some being put off by too many "foreign language" signs and menus in restaurants as well as the inconvenient bus routes from where they lived. The most frequented places were the markets and commercial areas such as Narantuul Market, Khuchit Shonkhor Market, and the third and fourth districts. The interviews evidenced the fact that the ger districts are a distinct urban entity of Ulaanbaatar, within which residents predominantly are employed, educated, and shop while visits to the countryside or the city center are primarily for recreation and pleasure.

The ger districts, therefore, are a unique typology: unlike the favelas they are not illegal settlements; unlike the Chinese urban villages they develop without necessary infrastructural services of sanitation or water supply and have very different dynamics between the urban and rural in terms of economic exchange. As with any urban settlement, it is more constructive to locate the specific forces, processes, and spatial characteristics than to attempt a definition within received terms like suburb, exurb, peri-urban, informal, or slum. The ger districts are none of the above; how to enable a transformation process that reacts to their specificity remains the key focus of investigation.

MASTER PLANS
Given the complexity of land tenure and the issues facing the ger districts, implementing master plans has proven difficult. The 2020 master plan for the city, which was formulated by the Japan International Cooperation Agency (JICA), was approved by parliament in 2002 and pushed for the creation of new satellite cities, a new airport, and an underground metro. Its cost was estimated at $16 billion.[80] Infrastructural funding was to be provided through the 2012 Chinggis Bond, a sovereign bond of $1.5 billion, with the intention to encourage capital investment through private developers.[81] The collapse of the commodities markets (2008–11) amid the global economic slowdown meant that developers were put off from potentially slow projects involving multiple negotiations with stakeholders

for low returns. In response, the 2020 master plan was amended in 2013 into a new vision, called Development Approaches 2030,[82] that emphasized the need to integrate the ger areas into the city through the creation of four strategic subcenters.

The redevelopment plans under the 2013 master plan revisions are being undertaken through the Asian Development Bank (ADB). Mongolia currently has upwards of $3.31 billion in loans, grants, and technical assistance commitments from the ADB, with $375.49 million allocated for "Water and Other Urban Infrastructure and Services," which includes ger district redevelopment.[83] The ADB-financed Urban Transport Development Investment Program involves the creation of a Bus Rapid Transport system (BRT) with new bus lanes that will transect the city connecting the four new subcenters to the city center. The subcenters will be developed through another ADB project, the Ger Areas Development Investment Program (GADIP), which will provide $320 million for infrastructure including heating, water, and sewerage. It will also improve roads and public services, and develop capacity for businesses and expanded economic opportunity. In turn, the Ulaanbaatar Green Affordable Housing and Resilient Urban Renewal Sector Project (AHURP) will create eco-districts at these subcenters containing 10,000 housing units in a model mixed-use community comprising 15 percent social, 55 percent affordable, and 30 percent market-rate housing together with public amenities and open spaces. The eco-districts plan proposes to increase the current household density by 3.6 times and sets environmental criteria for thermal performance and energy consumption, with a minimum apartment size of 35 square meters. In preparation, multiple stakeholder workshops conducted by consultants M.A.D. Investment Solutions, part of the ADB team, have taken place to ascertain the market value of the land based on whether owners have improved their plots, built houses, operate businesses, or rent their land. The mechanism for implementation will be through voluntary land swaps, and at the two initial sub-projects the ADB has confirmed agreements in principle from 72.5 percent of residents at Selbe East and 83.8 percent of residents at Bayankhoshuu West.[84] It has also attempted to adjust the development model to appeal to ger district residents by allowing residents access to land, providing greenhouses, and incorporating business spaces at the ground floor of buildings. Financial tools have been reworked to encourage private developers to participate in the project delivery, and attractive mortgage rates will be offered by chanelling Green Climate Fund loans through the commercial banks. The strategy is to limit the risk for investors as much as possible. Ultimately, however, the success of the project is contingent on private developers and contractors.

The above passage enumerates the entanglement of all of the different "tranches" of development that the ADB breaks into separate, but interrelated, pieces. The relentless acronyms, complexity of team structures involving multiple cross-disciplinary experts from around the world, and ability for projects to be updated or superseded makes it difficult to parse exactly what is going on at any one time. No doubt the information presented above is already out of date. However, this is the current modality of ger district development, predicated on loans from the ADB

This is the current modality of ger district development, predicated on loans from the ADB to the Mongolian government that will ultimately have to be paid back.

to the Mongolian government that will ultimately have to be paid back. This ultimately will stretch the stabilization of Mongolia's economy, which already in 2016 was reported to have $8.5 billion in external sovereign debt (up from $2 billion just a half decade earlier in 2010).[85] Additionally, the uncertainty of the currency conversion from the Green Climate Fund loans supporting the projects in US dollars to the local banks in Mongolian tugriks means that the promised low interest rates are not as low as originally anticipated.[86]
The COVID-19 pandemic has also created huge delays on the implementation of these projects. In 2021, the cost of construction materials was inflated 30-40 percent compared to 2019 prices, owing to supply shortages after the borders were closed to trade from January 2020 to July 2021.[87]

If successfully delivered, the interconnected ADB projects will bring much-needed improvement to the designated subcenters—the aim being to benefit 400,000 residents. However, the extent of the problems affecting the ger districts means that this still leaves approximately 440,000 ger district residents who live outside of these zones, lacking basic urban services and still contributing to toxic levels of air and soil pollution.
As these areas continue to grow, a different mechanism of ger district development must be conceived to address the increasingly threatening urban risks associated with this form of settlement.

DESIGN LOGICS
The next sections of the book propose a different model of ger district development. This includes built and unbuilt prototypes and a strategic approach to urban growth that harnesses incremental transformation as an alternative to the failure of the master plan. This model has emerged by developing an understanding of the ger districts from spatial analysis, household surveys, and through direct involvement in the process of design and construction. Through building, one confronts the immediacy of the issues at stake: negotiations with stakeholders and government officials, affordability, limitations of construction techniques and material sources, and the extreme climatic conditions.

The contextual overview as presented over the preceding pages provides an understanding of the forces that shape Ulaanbaatar's contemporary urban condition. The two paradigmatic shifts, to Soviet state control and to the post-revolution free-market, have radically reshaped life in both the countryside and the city. The hardships brought about by the transition into the liberal economy and collapse of the Soviet support structure led many to give up herding and move to the city—some drawn by hopes for a new prosperity fuelled by the promises of the extractive economy, others by better education and healthcare. As a result, the ger districts continue to expand rapidly each year. The fact that the poorest residents of the city own the majority of the land makes Ulaanbaatar a unique situation that requires a specific spatial response. As landowners, ger district residents are positioned to transform their land however they wish. Guiding this process towards more sustainable modes of development, introducing affordable typologies, and repairing and augmenting infrastructure and public programs is critical to our work there.

As these areas continue to grow, a different mechanism of ger district development must be conceived to address the increasingly threatening urban risks associated with this form of settlement.

Through building, one confronts the immediacy of the issues at stake: negotiations with stakeholders and government officials, affordability, limitations of construction techniques and material sources, and the extreme climatic conditions.

Urban Core	Pre - 1950
Communist Masterplan	1950 - 1990
Free Market Transition	1990 - 2002
Post - Land Claim Law	2002 - Present

The different phases of growth of the city, 1950–20.

I was born in Arkhangai aimag center, I am the eldest of two. After sixth grade, when I was thirteen, our family moved to Ulaanbaatar. The four of us moved to the capital, and the change was very difficult for me. I lived in a place where there were only dirt roads and there was always a lot of dust around. Also, close to where we lived, there was a waste collection area and all the rubbish trucks moving around created a lot of dust in the air. Back in Arkhangai aimag, we didn't have this kind of air pollution.

Chantsaldulm
Byambatseren

PROTO

TYP ING

The construction of the Ger Innovation Hub involving architecture students from Hong Kong and local residents, June 2018.

BUILDING
AS RESEARCH

Ulaanbaatar's deleterious post-1990 urbanization process has demonstrated top-down planning to be an ineffective tool for dealing with the spatial problems that confound territories in various stages of becoming urban. In such conditions an alternative approach is necessary in order to pivot the urbanization process towards a more sustainable future. Our objective in working in the ger districts of Ulaanbaatar is to affirm the agency of the architect in this process. In the gaps and inadequacies created by master plans, the architect can play a critical role in shaping the city. To do so, the urban should not be thought of as a singular scale but instead as a dynamic process occurring across multiple scales. Buildings have the capacity to transform the city when they operate not as singular objects but as *typologies:* spatial organizations that can adapt and evolve alongside the emerging conditions of which they are part. Typologies register the evolution of historical change in buildings, and thus they can be documented, classified, analyzed, and used as a body of knowledge for architects.[88] Typologies evolve according to specific contextual constraints including climate, resources, technology, or programmatic demands. As those contexts change, typologies either adapt or become obsolete.

As a site that is becoming urban, Ulaanbaatar's ger districts have undergone processes of change predominantly through the application of the vernacular ger and the generic single-family house—two typologies that have given rise to a pattern of extensive and problematic urbanization. Neither typology addresses the specific challenges that have arisen in the city's urban transformation. In fact, they have contributed to those issues with the speedy territorial expansion made possible through the affordability and reproducibility of the ger, and the inability of either typology to address the needs for densification or the provision of infrastructure. Both typologies are intrinsically not urban, having emerged from nonurban contexts of the nomadic steppe and the rural or suburban setting of the private villa. They exist as objects within a plot that do not give rise to any models of how a city fabric, including its infrastructure and public spaces, can be organized. They do not have the capacity to change or to be configured differently when clustered together, instead always duplicating the same set of spatial relationships. Thus unable to anticipate growth, these typologies cannot be part of a spatial strategy that promotes densification and the organization of the public realm. The example of Ulaanbaatar shows that the application of these known typologies is counterproductive to creating a sustainable and liveable urban settlement. However, this example also demonstrates a clear correlation between typology and urban development—that is, typologies alter, shape, and define urban growth.

TYPOLOGICAL DESIGN

Typologies are defined by their spatial organization—the core diagram or spatial code that makes them unique. They are not characterised by function, which can change over time. In this way, typologies pertain to the core disciplinary pursuit of architecture: the formation and organization of space. The evolution of typology, or building type, and its use as a design tool is clearly articulated in Rafael Moneo's 1978 essay "On Typology."[89] Moneo questions the relevance of type and its historical contribution to architectural discourse, concluding that the problem of type remains a fundamental question for contemporary architecture. Moneo contends, on the one hand, that modernism's rejection of type as too restrictive for the pursuit of abstract space can be seen as a failure to address the city. On the other hand, for architects such as Aldo Rossi, historical type became the origin for all future articulations of architecture and its relation to the urban, yet ultimately this too is limited and trapped by a nostalgia for a city that no longer exists. More than forty years on, these two opposing positions on the role of typology and its relation to the contemporary city are increasingly relevant to discuss.

Rossi reclaimed architectural history as the core driver of the discipline and of his own design process. For him, such reclamation is possible through typology as the vehicle to embody the historical evolution of architecture and its potential to create continuity of urban form.[90] This urban form and its constituent typologies are positioned within an ideal city—a conditional and abstracted context in which to work. Rossi's approach thus connects architecture back to the city and distinguishes the role of the architect as working towards urban continuity rather than its erasure and complete formal reinvention, as was advocated by his modernist predecessors. However, the approach is predicated on the idea that there is already a predetermined set of typological conditions that can meet the needs and challenges of the contemporary city. In the Italian context in which Rossi was primarily working, historical layers of typological evolution indeed are ever present, such that his historically

Typologies pertain to the core disciplinary pursuit of architecture: the formation and organization of space.

idealised version of the city can at least be imagined if not realized. In this sense, considering the pressures of urbanization, Rossi's position is divorced from the messy realities and conflicting negotiations that one faces in the contemporary global city. Processes of urbanization in other contexts, particularly those lacking a deep architectural and urban history or an origin from which to attempt any such form of urban continuity, render such an approach unrealistic. Rossi's approach furthermore presupposes that all solutions to typological change and evolution originate from the core knowledge of architectural history itself. In cases such as Ulaanbaatar, however, existing typologies are not able to address the complexity of the urban transformation process nor the contextual constraints of climate, economy, and cultural specificity. Instead, these contextual issues require the creation of new typologies, which not only can address the needs of a particular city but also can be conceived to adapt to future change, and to shape it.

In contrast to the typological design method of Rossi, modern architecture in the first half of the twentieth century unburdened itself from history and along with it the necessity of typology. Instead of typology, the modernist quest for industrial and technological advancement in architecture focused on the invention of prototypes. Prototypes became the vehicle to realize the dreams of architectural mass-production, of the transformation of building into product, and, as Le Corbusier polemicised in 1923, of the house as "a machine for living in."[91] An industrial design process geared towards prefabrication and mass consumption, prototyping was co-opted by architects such as Jean Prouvé, Walter Gropius, Konrad Wachsmann, and Buckminster Fuller to develop architecture as a technological and commercial product. For example, both Prouvé's Demountable House (1944) and Gropius and Wachsmann's Packaged House (1944) concern the creation of prefabricated engineered components that can be easily assembled on site. The design of the joint—specifically its ability to withstand load, allow for variation, and lock components together—became a dominant research investigation and led to many patent applications. The Packaged House was patented in the United States in 1944, emphasizing the uniqueness of the four-way metal Wedge Connector. The design patent for an entire building such as this represents a significant shift: from architecture as something that can be openly copied and transformed by others, as in the case of typological change, to something that is replicated, manufactured, and intellectually protected by a company structure.[92] Nonetheless, in many examples the knowledge of the prototype could not successfully transfer into scalable and profitable production. Gropius and Wachsmann set up the General Panel Corporation in 1942 to manufacture and commercialise their designs, but the disruption of the Second World War, high production costs, and a lack of both significant sales and injections of capital resulted in the company's liquidation in 1951.[93]

Preceding these examples of factory-made building components, Le Corbusier's Maison Dom-Ino of 1914 combines top-down and bottom-up construction methods. It is neither evolved from a preexisting house typology nor developed to be mass-produced in a single factory.

In cases such as Ulaanbaatar, however, existing typologies are not able to address the complexity of the urban transformation process nor the contextual constraints of climate, economy, and cultural specificity. Instead, these contextual issues require the creation of new typologies, which not only can address the needs of a particular city but also can be conceived to adapt to future change, and to shape it.

Its origins lie, rather, in the spatial logic of the continuous assembly-line factory floor made possible by the structural properties of the reinforced concrete frame.[94] The resilience of the Dom-Ino over the one hundred-plus years since its invention—as evidenced by its global proliferation regardless of cultural, social, or environmental specificity—is made possible by the combination of the ready supply worldwide of cement and steel from large-scale industrial suppliers, which allows for the creation of a robust structural-concrete frame and slab, and the open-ended, insitu infill that can be completed with locally available materials and labor.[95] Together, these two distinct aspects of construction create a building system that is incredibly versatile in its capability to change scale and to be configured according to residents' choices for their domestic space, while still maintaining a constant underlying spatial organization.

Le Corbusier's Dom-Ino was designed to have no horizontal beams and with the columns placed flush at the short sides and recessed on the long edges to allow for its continuous horizontal expansion and growth along a continuous line.[96] The adapted, more commonplace version operates simply as a gridded frame for infill facades and interior walls, with individual houses usually placed separately from each other. Thanks to the aforementioned global supply chain of relatively low-cost cement and reinforcement material, this generic Dom-Ino has become widespread as well as culturally and climatically indistinct. The Dom-Ino prototype has evolved into a typology.

In rural China, a combination of government construction grants and increasing remittances sent to villagers from family members in urban areas has resulted in many families replacing their traditional mud-brick homes with concrete frame houses.[97] In other cases, the mechanism of urbanization is through infrastructure and economic imperatives. Jiaoxi, a village on the periphery of Changsha, Hunan Province, is a case-study site where we have researched a process of village relocation caused by the construction of a highway together with new economic development zones to incentivise urbanization. In the process, villages and farmland are bisected and redeveloped, for which villagers are compensated financially. Most of them choose to reinvest this money to build five-to six-story concrete-frame houses that can additionally host income-generating programs like shops, guest rooms, or karaoke bars. The case study indicates the readiness of villagers to build in anticipation of financial gains created by the highway, and their preferred construction method of the Dom-Ino concrete frame and infill. Propelled by such factors as the highway network's growth of 750 percent since 1970 and the government's intent to have reclassified 100 million rural dwellers into urban citizens by 2020, the rate of urbanization across China is estimated at 2 billion square meters of buildings per year.[98] The prevailing model that fulfils this huge demand for modernisation, allows for adaptation to multiple uses, and is cheap, is the mutated form of the Dom-Ino, arguably making it the most ubiquitous model for affordable housing around the world. Yet because the Dom-Ino typology has no specific relation to its environment, its ubiquitous construction often results in overly dense districts that lack basic provisions of sanitation or public space and perform inadequately in environmental terms, as evidenced by many informal settlements worldwide in areas that are rapidly urbanising; Rocinha in Rio De Janiero,[99] Manshiyat Naser in Cairo,[100] and Savda Ghevra in Delhi[101] are just three of the most prominent examples.

In contrast to the one-size-fits-all urbanization of the Dom-Ino typology, Frank Lloyd Wright's design experiments with the Usonian House and Usonian Automatic (1936–58) offer an alternative perspective on the role of prototyping and typological change. For Wright, the imperative to create affordable housing was bound with a concern for heating, lighting, and sanitation. His series of Usonian House designs are highly specific in their plan, relationship to site, and spatial form, but nonetheless share an underlying logic of organization and construction. Wright built over 50 Usonian Houses that all share in a radically shifted spatial organization of the single-family house through the integration of the kitchen, which he dubbed the workspace, into the dining and living space of the house. The Usonian House thus has typological potential. Specifically, in the coherence of its spatial organization lies the potential to generate multiple variations of plan-form based on the specific climate and terrain of a site.[102]

Wright embedded environmental systems into the construction of his Usonian Houses, developing a radiant heat system of underfloor heating elements. The construction system adapted to economic constraints of each period. The prewar Usonian used timber "sandwich" panels and integrated furniture, removing the need for additional plastering and painting of interior finishes. During the postwar period the costs of material and labor increased, so Wright devised the Usonian Automatic building system. This consisted of a specialised concrete block that could be threaded with reinforcement bar and then cast together with concrete in situ. The system was used for walls and the roof and was organized on a grid based on the unit dimensions of the block. Unlike the prototypical development of a singular product intended for industrial mass production, the Usonian Automatic is a prototype for a building system that allows for multiple variations.[103]

PROTOTYPING TYPOLOGIES: A DESIGN PROCESS
The history of prototyping and typological design for affordable housing offers conceptual and practical lessons to the case of Ulaanbaatar. For one, it shows a clear correlation between typological change and urban transformation: to change patterns of growth, new typologies need to be introduced and proliferated. Prototypes generated towards mass production have demonstrated architecture's resistance to becoming a commodified product. A universal system furthermore cannot suffice to meet the contemporary challenges of climate change or the social and cultural demands particular to a place, so typological change needs to embed ideas of environmental systems and the capacity for local specificity. Nevertheless, the built prototype is a vital research tool, helping to develop knowledge of a building's environmental and construction performance as well as generating feedback from residents to understand its potential for urban proliferation. A prototype is thus the precursor to the development of a new typology.

A universal system furthermore cannot suffice to meet the contemporary challenges of climate change or the social and cultural demands particular to a place, so typological change needs to embed ideas of environmental systems and the capacity for local specificity.

The process whereby a typology can be identified, designed, and tested for its ability to impact urban transformation is defined by us as *prototyping*.

The process whereby a typology can be identified, designed, and tested for its ability to impact urban transformation is defined by us as *prototyping*. It is a critical method of our work. We consider all prototypes as built experiments, allowing for feedback and adjustment to improve their performance, leading to the potential incremental evolution into a typology. Not all prototypes become typologies. Some become obsolete or remain dormant until the conditions of the context change to be receptive to taking up the prototype as a typology. Others simply fail, yet their failure forces the project to pivot to new directions both conceptually and strategically, for example, working with a completely different structural or material system. Many remain as one-off pilot projects that nevertheless reveal underlying logics of the urban context in which they are located. In this way prototyping is a research method that produces new knowledge about a location and how to design within it. Our intention is to develop prototypes that can become typologies—to instigate typological change and transform the process of urbanization through architecture.

As a design method that approaches urban transformation through the introduction of new typologies, prototyping radically differs from the methods of urban design and planning, with their prescriptions of a general layout, composition, and organization of built form and infrastructure.

As a design method that approaches urban transformation through the introduction of new typologies, prototyping radically differs from the methods of urban design and planning, with their prescriptions of a general layout, composition, and organization of built form and infrastructure. As already demonstrated, these methods have proven ineffective in rapidly developing yet impoverished conditions like Ulaanbaatar. Amidst the continued efforts of such top-down planning, the self-built, generic version of the Dom-Ino has become the dominant model of affordable housing in informal settlements.

The Dom-Ino, Usonian Houses, and Usonian Automatic provide insights that can guide an approach to the design of prototypes, such as: considering how top-down construction systems can combine with local methods of assembly as in the Dom-Ino; developing a spatial organization that can adapt to specific site conditions as in the Usonian Houses and creating building systems developed around affordability with embedded systems for sanitation and thermal performance as in Usonian Automatic. Such basic principles have led us to define prototypes with the following criteria:

> *Prototypes* have a unique spatial organization and underlying logic. They are spatial generators that originate multiple variations from their fundamental organizational diagrams. This makes them robust in their ability to be altered in size, material, and aesthetic characteristics while maintaining their underlying spatial code. If the diagram is lost, or becomes illegible or confused, the prototype has become something else.

> *Prototypes* are not singular one-offs but have the capacity to proliferate. They do not proliferate through replication but are designed to adapt and be altered by specific site conditions such as terrain, aspect, material resources, programming, availability of labor, economy, or social and cultural living customs.

Prototypes are built experiments, allowing feedback from stakeholders and evaluation of their technical performance. The design of prototypes is iterative and informed by feedback, with each new model improving upon and developing from past versions.

Prototypes can inform an understanding about the underlying forces acting on an urban system including local policy, governance, the actions of stakeholders, and other emerging developments impacting transformation. This mode of working with prototypes makes them especially valuable research tools.

Prototypes are designed from conception with specific knowledge of their particular site. In this regard they are not ideal models devoid of the unique pressures acting on a context but rather are underpinned with knowledge of the current processes and spatial form of urban transformation, existing models of development, and how residents live currently as well as their needs for the future. Our typological approach sets up parallel processes of research and design that become interlinked through prototyping.

Although the moment when a prototype becomes instilled as a typology remains a test of time and question of its overall proliferation, the prototyping phase provides indicators of which test cases are more equipped to become typology. The following examples for a waste collection point, a community center, and an affordable house demonstrate this method and the ambition to initiate typological change. They also present various outcomes of the prototyping method, whether as productive failure, one-off pilot, or something close to initiating its assimilation as a new typology. In the process of their design, construction, and evaluation, which has been ongoing since we started working in Mongolia in 2014, these projects have enabled us to reflect critically on our definition of *prototype* and on our working methods. This process also situates our work within the disciplinary discourse of typology and its capacity to inform and engage contemporary urbanization.

The waste collection point in
Khan-Uul 13 nearing completion,
January 2015.

PRODUCTIVE FAILURE: ADAPTIVE INFRASTRUCTURE FOR URBAN WASTE COLLECTION

March 2015: We arrived at our project site in the outlying ger district Khoroo of Khan-Uul 13. At the time, Google Street View showed the project nearing completion—an incision into the landscape, part earthwork, part architecture. A concrete, wedge-shaped wall retained a sloped earthen mound to create a hidden infrastructure and meeting place. This was a digital ghost. In reality, we showed up to only face a snow-covered pile of rubble and a dog carcass.

Rewind to February 2014: our very first trip to Mongolia. At this moment the city was in a precarious stage of transformation. Although excessive GDP growth rates after the discovery of vast reserves of coal, copper, and gold had caused wild speculation and investment promises in 2011, by 2014 the cost of extraction, political stalemates with mining companies, and the decreased value of commodities led to a stagnation of development. At the same time, the expansion of the ger districts was having detrimental effects on the entire city, most acutely the debilitating levels of air pollution. The consciousness that the ger districts were becoming an urgent problem was very present, particularly amongst international NGOs and development organizations.

I was first made aware of this context after my wife returned from Ulaanbaatar on a business trip. Her descriptions of the city as an extreme and unique condition of felt tents, concrete apartment blocks, and glassy towers amidst a frontier-town atmosphere was intriguing and also presented a pertinent context to explore. My previous work with Rural Urban Framework, a design research lab based at the University of Hong Kong, had focused on the transformation of the Chinese countryside and how our built projects could address urgent social, educational, and environmental issues that had emerged in this process of change.[104] Ulaanbaatar represented a potential future research direction to build on this approach, to further innovate and test how architecture could impact urban transformation.

After a preliminary research phase, we arrived in the city with some basic knowledge of the key issues, a list of potential partners, and a booklet of ideas. These diagrammatic concepts each had a name, an objective, and a spatial organization. We met with as many people as we could to show them our proposals and discuss their potential. A meeting with The Asia Foundation, a non-profit international development organization, turned out to be particularly fruitful. The foundation's regional office in Ulaanbaatar was set up in 1990 following the democratic revolution. As the country has moved to a free-market economy, the foundation has addressed issues of transparency in governance, policy making, infrastructure, resource management, and the environment. A key project has been the production of an interactive community map of ger districts from data gathered through numerous meetings with residents. The map provides a database for local services such as bus stops, playgrounds, clinics, schools, and water kiosks. It also shows areas of illegal dumpsites alongside official sites for waste collection. For herders living in the countryside, resources originate from what is readily available: water from a stream; milk and meat from the herd; and dung for fuel. In the city, the impossibility of self-sufficiency and the consumption of readily available packaged goods produces excess plastic and metal waste. In the absence of adequate collection procedures, anything that cannot be burnt is disposed of in public spaces, water channels, or by the roadside. In contrast, individual *Khashaa* (plots) tend to be clean. The foundation's maps provided evidence of the most impacted locations and strategically where it would make sense to intervene.

In partnership with the Ulaanbaatar city government and with funding from the Australian Department for Foreign Affairs and Trade (DFAT), the project aimed to alter the policy and procedures of waste collection. This goal was to be achieved through three objectives: the creation of a clear schedule for waste collection, allowing residents to monitor and hold companies accountable if they had not collected at the agreed time; agreement upon new regulations to establish minimum service standards and regular performance reviews for collection companies; and the construction of three prototypes to test how collection facilities could be improved. The design and successful operation of the collection points also needed the cooperation and input from the end users. Those were the district leaders and residents of the selected sites, the Recycling Association who would manage and run the recycling office, the waste collection truck company, and the mayor's office.

The foundation named the project Smart Collection Points because to be a success it would have to navigate several levels including the physical waste-collection building, neighborhood participation and outreach, the scheduling of trucks, and city-wide policy changes from the mayor's office to change the administration of waste collection in these areas. In our first meeting, we presented ideas for five prototypes to address a range of urgent issues. One, named Attractor Core, involved creating a community hub that could be integrated into the residents' daily routine: a place to deposit waste rubbish, take a shower, buy supplies, eat, sit and read, collect water, and then return home. The foundation was drawn to this concept, and we were tasked to develop the prototype that would be piloted and constructed on three sites. The prototype would contain a drop off point for residents to deposit their waste, an collection point for the trucks, an area for collecting and sorting recyclables, and an improved public space. The goal was to design and construct the projects within the next nine months, prior to November 2014 when the harsh winter would make construction impracticable.

ADAPTING AND SITUATING

The spatial organization of the prototype was designed to use a ramp to order the process of collection. Our idea was to integrate the process of waste disposal into the everyday routine of residents. Infrastructurally, it was a place to drop off waste with space for a recycling center where plastic bottles, metal cans, and glass could be received, sorted, and collected. The ramp was an extension of existing routes to the water kiosk or the bus stop. It also provided a place to pause, a public gathering space that, at a second stage and dependant on residents' needs, could become a playground or a basketball court. This idea was taken from our observations of the water kiosks, where we saw how the daily routine of water collection makes the kiosks places where people meet and chat, the only really collective, public space in the districts.

Based on the mapping exercise of The Asia Foundation and input from the mayor's office, we were given three sites to situate and adapt the concept diagram based on the particular constraints of each location. The sites were in three different ger sub districts, or Khoroo's: Bayanzurkh-27, a central ger area close to the city accessed only by dirt roads; Chingeltei-16, a mid ger area next to a paved road; and Khan-Uhl-13, a fringe ger area located at the periphery of the city. In June 2014, we visited and analyzed each site, and made stakeholder presentations to local khesig leaders, representatives from the mayor's office, and local waste collection truck operators. The site at Bayanzurkh-27 was steep and contained loose soil. We were told that this was from recent illegal dumping and could be excavated. The site bounded a ravine that had a natural spring within 50 meters of the proposed collection point, so we had to ensure this would not be polluted by our building or any of the waste collection programs. Based on our observations on site, the design progressed to take advantage of the slope, with an upper floor containing a community event space connected to a ramp leading down to the collection area located at the landing and further descending to the recycling facility below. Chingeltei-16's site was the uneven, sloped dirt terrain of a verge on the side of a recently constructed road. The scheme here was adapted to take advantage of the topography to form a ramp leading from high ground down to the road that contained several places for rubbish drop-off. The recycling station was contained under the upper two of the ramp's three switch backed sections, while the lower two hinged apart to create an open public space. The site at Khan-Uul 13 had a different character from the other two. The plots were much larger and the population quite sparse. Residents still kept animals. The dirt roads were simply the paths most travelled by vehicles. Our intent was to create an artificial topography in this flat land. The design called for excavating 1.5 meters (4.9 foot) below ground for the collection and infilling 1.5 meters (4.9 foot) above ground for the drop off, with a retaining-wall barrier holding this new mound in place.

The structure for all three projects was to be reinforced concrete with a minimum thickness of 150 millimeters, a dimension selected based on availability of materials, cost, and also fire regulations. As many residents in the ger districts deposit ash waste into collection points, fire is an ever-present hazard, so the drop-off point need to be as contained as possible, constructed from non-combustible materials, and located as far away from any houses as the site would allow. Glazing was to be kept at a minimum owing both to its cost and danger of being smashed. We therefore decided on creating small circular apertures only into occupied areas. These would be created in the walls by casting the concrete around PVC pipes placed in the formwork and setting the glazing on the interior side.

July and August were intense months of back and forth between us and the local architect in Ulaanbaatar, who was responsible for the submission drawings and the regulatory requirements. After receiving initial costs, The Asia Foundation asked us to drastically economize through changes to size, materials, removal of courtyard paving finishes, landscaping, exterior lighting, and the amount of glazing. Furthermore, after the amount of excavation required at Bayanzurkh was deemed too costly, we abandoned the site altogether and proceeded only with Chingeltei and Khan-Uul.

We were advised in early September that the mayor's office had agreed to split the construction costs with The Asia Foundation. The revised schemes and detailed drawings were completed and ready for submission to the municipality's Urban Development Agency for expertise approval by mid-September. With the city now a financial stakeholder, there was hope that the approval could be expedited and that the city would directly appoint a contractor in one week rather than the typical two, yet the timeframe turned out differently and dragged into October. By that time the temperature was already plummeting below zero. We were concerned we were out of time.

Then everything went quiet—we did not hear anything from the Asia Foundation for over a month and assumed the project was dead. In mid-November the foundation reported in an email, *"It may not be possible anymore to construct this year and next year we will no longer have the budget for this purpose."* This was devastating for us—after nearly nine months of intensive work it appeared likely that the project would remain unbuilt. Shortly thereafter, we received another email: *"There has been some development regarding construction of the sites this year. The Mayor's Office have finalised contracts with two construction companies in the last week or so who will use anti-freeze construction methods."* This was very positive news, we thought at the time. On December 3, only three days after receiving notice that the city had agreed on contracts with two contractors, one for Chingeltei and the other for Khan-Uul, we were sent photographs from the construction sites. Were surprised to see that at both sites the foundations had been poured and the formwork for the walls was being set up. We immediately arranged a site visit for the following week.

At both sites the contractors made small fires on the ground within the building footprint to thaw the earth so that it could be excavated. The temperature during the day was around -15°C (5°F), making construction arduous. To cast the concrete each contractor had to add antifreeze to the cement so that the water would not freeze before it could cure. We found the concrete quality to be poor at both sites and were concerned about its structural integrity. At Khan-Uul there even were gaps in the retaining wall between one pour and the next.

After returning from the site visit, on December 23 we received additional photographs and a report from the Asia Foundation's client representative, Delgebayer Badam. At Chingeltei, we saw, the contractor had selected an ornamental panelled door. We immediately rejected the door and asked for it to be replaced. This door became a personal affront, an attack on our architectural integrity and belief in 'good' design. We argued and fought, providing options to make this aberration go away. The Asia Foundation was not nearly as alarmed and let us know in no uncertain terms that if we were so bothered by the door we should pay for its replacement ourselves. Their priority was completing the project so that it could begin operation, as Tirza Theunissen, the foundation's deputy country representative, articulated in email to us on December 29: *"This is Mongolia and people do not always respect decisions that have been made ... From our and our City counterpart's perspective, we are satisfied with the Chingeltei collection point and want to proceed with the awareness raising and experimenting with the use which was the main reason why we undertook this project as part of our solid waste management work. Being able to demonstrate use by the community and impact on overall collection is crucial for us. With less than 3 months to go in terms of implementation of our urban services project before we start winding down, we need to now proceed."*

Construction then extended into January as temperatures continued to drop. A February trip to Ulaanbaatar proved critical. At both sites, an inspection of the concrete revealed patches of solid ice. This indicated that the water in the concrete had not cured but simply had frozen due to insufficient antifreeze in the cement mixture. In our meeting with the project manager from the mayor's office we went through all the items on the defects list. It became apparent that the contractor at Chingeltei had already been paid over 80 percent of the contract sum, and the project manager speculated that it would be difficult to persuade the contractor to rectify the work. He also added that he had received many complaints from the contractor on the escalating costs of winter construction. It was agreed by all parties that incorrect and potentially unsafe work needed

A truck collects waste from the collection point that is located opposite the bus stop connecting residents to the city center. 2015.

to be made good and the project manager agreed to set up a meeting with Toonto Grand, the local architect, as well as the contractors and The Asia Foundation, to plan next steps. From that point, despite our work to help repair the construction defects, the Asia Foundation curtailed correspondence with us. Delgerbayer, their local representative, and their project manager both left the organization. Theunissen did not reply to our emails requesting updates on the repairs. After many attempts to contact members of the team, we received an email from Delgerbayer, who wrote, "*I understand that Khan Uul SCP [Smart Collection Point] roof is broken down due to winter casting and cement quality.*" The warming spring temperatures had melted the ice in the concrete and the roof had collapsed—the reason behind the mound of rubble we would witness on our visit in March. Khan-Uhl was an abject failure. Chingeltei-16, however, was intact and ready for operation.

PRODUCTIVE FAILURE, ONE YEAR LATER
We visited the project at Chingeltei-16 again February 2016 and found rubbish strewn across all surfaces of the ramp. Instead of placing the trash through the steel flaps, residents simply were dumping their garbage on the pathway of the ramp. The doors to the recycling center were unhinged and inside the collection area the walls were charred black, evidence of a fire probably caused by cinders from stove-ash. We called the Kheseg leaders, who arranged a cleanup. The next day we arrived at the same time as the truck collecting the rubbish. The workers shovelled the trash into the truck as residents meandered down the now clean walkway. The project was how we envisaged it. A few months later, the recycling company was operating, collecting and sorting cans and bottles as we had anticipated. A year later, the door that had caused us so much consternation was locked and no one knew where the key was. The city had started to organize household collection and so the structure became programmatically obsolete.

As we continue to conduct research in Ulaanbaatar, most times we are there we make a pilgrimage of sorts to the site. Every time we visit, I am convinced that the structure could be made to work, not necessarily as a waste collection point, but adapted as a shop or a youth club. A basketball half-court could be added, the entire structure could be painted as a collective art project, and trees could be planted in the inner courtyard. The structure was designed to be robust, to withstand changes in program and to adapt and evolve based on the demands of the district. Yet the *project* could not evolve. It became constrained by a lack of ownership and management. The Asia Foundation didn't want to deal with it. From their perspective the project was finished, the funding spent, the reporting done. The mayor's office had a new set of civil servants after the election in July 2016, and to them this was someone else's idea for which they didn't want to be responsible. Nor would they hand it over to the residents or Kheseg leaders.

Was the building's failure that of the architecture or of the architect? If indeed the underlying method was at fault, could the agency of the architect be conceived of differently? During the project we acted in a conventional mode of architectural practice—we responded to a client brief, we made designs, and we tried to manage the construction as best we could. We were subservient to other forces acting on the project: the inability of the NGO client to extend their funding window to avoid winter construction; the lack of clear ownership and involvement of the city to manage the project; and a missed opportunity to activate local residents as stakeholders. Our misguided urge to 'correct' the ornamental door reflected an architect's instinct to rectify bad taste. It would be nicer with a better door, but this was not the core of the project. We should have considered more carefully which aspects of the project needed to be so tightly controlled. Such an attitude needed to be incorporated into not only our working method but also how we conceived and designed the project from its inception. In essence, the problem was less about architectural form and space and more about architectural practice and its process.

In essence, the problem was less about architectural form and space and more about architectural practice and its process.

The waste collection points were designed as prototypes that could adapt programmatically and according to specific site conditions. However, the project lacked a concomitant agency embedded within prototyping as a method, thus it failed to build up a network of stakeholders with a vested and continued interest in making the project a success. Prototyping, in how we now define it as a specific method, must enable the construction of a constellation of empowered actors.

In order for this or any other prototype to become a typology, it would require further development in two seemingly contradictory directions. On the one hand, typologies must be autonomous: they must exist independently from clients or city administrations and be able to withstand the vagaries of circumstantial changes such as the election of different local officials or a reliance on singular funding structures. In this way they are both robust and adaptable, able to withstand changes in program whilst maintaining their core spatial organization. On the other hand, typologies are not defined by formal and organizational autonomy alone. To evolve from a prototype to a typology, the project would need to develop a deeper situatedness, being specifically of a place, rooted both to its past and to its future. The duality between autonomy and locality is a productive tension that can create the conditions for a typology to emerge and proliferate.

To evolve from a prototype to a typology, the project would need to develop a deeper situatedness, being specifically of a place, rooted both to its past and to its future.

The Waste Collection Points were our first built projects in Mongolia. The process revealed the challenges and the harsh realities of construction, procurement, finance, and climate. It heightened our awareness of the importance of the network of collaborators needed to initiate, undertake, and maintain a project for it to succeed. Reflecting on that process enabled us to rethink how prototyping could become more of a working method rather than a way to conceptualise just the object we were creating. This shift altered how we conceived of the agency of the architect. We didn't want to have clients. We didn't want to depend on other people's budgets. We didn't want to be a service provider. We wanted to design an ecology of practice.

In September 2019, four years after completion, the entire structure was being used as a dumping site for waste.

The collection point in 2022 being used as a community recycling facility.

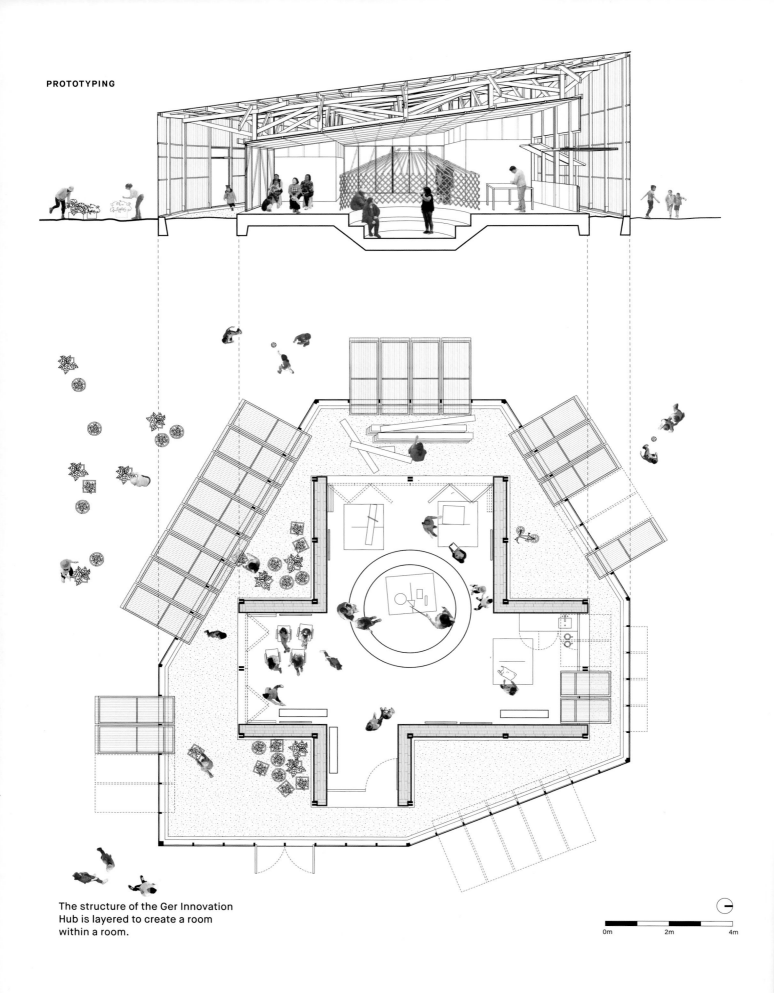

The structure of the Ger Innovation
Hub is layered to create a room
within a room.

0m   2m   4m

ENABLING COMMUNITY

After the difficulties we encountered with the waste collection points, we continued to actively engage in the ger districts. We shifted our focus to deepen our understanding of the mechanisms underlying the growth of the settlements in order to better position design strategies that could change future patterns of the urbanization process there. We made this research the subject and focus of architectural studios we taught at the University of Hong Kong in 2016 and at Columbia University in 2017. The studios enabled us to conduct a parallel line of investigation that used the constraints of the conditions as a springboard to generate more speculative design projects. They also provided an opportunity to become more engaged with the community by conducting fieldwork, household interviews, and workshops with local people to get feedback on proposals. The fieldtrips and workshops provided energy and momentum to the project that otherwise might have been lost without a definitive building commission.

The first workshop was in the winter of 2016 in a primary school in Sukhbaatar-16, involving combined groups of residents and students drawing and sketching over three different scaled aerial photos of the district, highlighting ideas for scenarios of future change. The second workshop, in the summer of 2016, was a collaboration with a vocational training school, the Institute of Engineering and Technology (IET), in which we designed and built the timber structure of a housing prototype that could plug into a ger. Critical to the success of these trips was the involvement and collaboration of Badruun Gardi and Enkhjin Batjargal. We had met them both on our very first trip to Ulaanbaatar in 2014, when they were working at the Zorig Foundation, an NGO set up to pursue democratic values in Mongolia. Badruun and Enkhjin assisted us during all of our trips and introduced us to other stakeholders working on ger district issues. Most importantly, they were both passionate about ger district issues and wanted to impact change. Badruun and Enkhjin, along with Dulguun Bayasgalan, became our core group of collaborators. All three were educated at international universities and had opportunities to remain abroad to pursue their careers, but instead chose to return to Mongolia to impact change in their home country.

Shortly after we began working together, Rural Urban Framework was invited to create an installation at the Venice Biennale of Architecture in 2016.[105] We designed a series of ger adaptations and used them as screening rooms for short documentary films Dulguun had made portraying people in the ger districts. Covering the daily life of a young couple living in a ger, a family of three who have built a house, a group of neighborhood kids, and an elderly man and his wife who moved from an apartment in the city to a ger, the films reflected the diversity of ger district dwellers both in terms of their family structure and their economic means. The exhibition was a mechanism to develop our research, which included experimenting with the tectonics of the ger. We tested how to hold up the central oculus using a cantilevered exterior truss, merging the existing vernacular structure with new timber construction. Through that experimentation an attitude developed about the latent potential of the ger to be the origin of transformation. Not only is the ger the only vernacular Mongolian architecture, it is emblematic of Mongolian identity.

In conversations, Badruun began to envisage an NGO that would formalise what we were already doing—organizing community workshops and collaborating on exhibitions—and work with other institutions and foundations to push innovative solutions for the ger districts. In 2016, Badruun and Enhkjin, together with new board members, co-founded the nonprofit social enterprise GerHub. A series of exhibitions followed where we continued to develop film narratives and test different spatial models of how to work with the ger. At the London Design Museum we subsumed the ger within a mass of felt, giving form to the negative space around the ger as a solid.[106] At MAAS in Sydney[107] we displayed a truss that extended from the ger to create an interstitial space with the potential to stitch several households together as a collective, shared space. As we worked GerHub also expanded. Initially based out of a coworking space in the center of the city, the organization hoped to deepen its engagement in the districts with a space where it could conduct workshops, education programs, and events. Enkhjin advocated for the urgent need to create public space and civic infrastructure in the districts, recognising the demand and desire from residents to have access to those resources. In navigating the shift from the autonomy of nomadic life, many residents face new challenges that affect a collective body of people rather than just individual households.

Rather than projecting our own predetermined idea of what would constitute community for residents, we sought out existing models within the ger districts to understand how we might address issues of living together and the lack of public resources. During our previous trips to the city, we had often visited Ulzii Sodnomsenge's initiative, called Green Lake, not far from our waste collection point at Chingeltei-12. Twenty years ago, Ulzii saw potential in an abandoned quarry. He cleaned it up and created a small lake, allowing people to rent boats in the summer and ice skate during winter. Subsequently, he has added small structures that have become a community resource—a place for reading and borrowing books, for music lessons, or for kids to play inside.

Green Lake became an example of how we could approach our project with GerHub, gradually building up awareness and trust, and creating new activities for people. The project also reinforced the need for residents to have somewhere to go during the winter other than their ger. Between November and March, the average temperature in Ulaanbaatar is -17°C (1.4°F), so most families are compelled to stay within their ger for all activities. Parents make younger children wear restraining harnesses to prevent them from touching scalding stoves or chimney pipes, even when they are present. Furthermore, the lack of access to childcare in the ger districts is an escalating issue, a symptom of the inability of government to provide civic infrastructure for a growing population covering an ever-widening geographic area. Only half of the 146,000 children between the ages of two and five in the ger districts will be allocated a kindergarten place.[108] This has led to the emergence of unregulated private childcare, district lotteries to select children, and reports of bribes to ensure a class spot.[109]

Independently from our work in Mongolia, we successfully applied for funding from the Hong Kong Jockey Club in 2017 to set up and implement design-build workshops in rural China with students from Hong Kong that would also include a follow-up trip so that students could see the impact of what they had achieved. The intention was to create collaborative teams of students from different educational backgrounds and give them an opportunity to travel outside of Hong Kong to build something together in a very different context, exposing them to challenging issues of habitation and development. Although initially planned for rural China, we decided to undertake two projects, one to renovate a vernacular Tulou in Fujian Province,[110] and the other focused on Ulaanbaatar, which the charity accepted.

Together with GerHub, we began to conceive of a building that would be rooted in the districts. It would open to residents and be the locus of all of GerHub's activities. The project was not conceived to fix singular problems such as the lack of childcare. Instead, it would be a place that allowed the organization to work with residents to collectively identify their most pressing needs and to assist them in finding the agency to act. For example, it could be space for afterschool homework clubs, a creche, or creative play workshops. The project was about enabling residents, with the support of GerHub, to address what it means to live together and to forge new methods of collaboration, to instil community building into the gradual process of urban acculturation. We named the project the Ger Innovation Hub. With the Jockey Club funding, we had the catalyst to initiate the design and realize part of the construction.

The completed Ger Innovation Hub
in winter, January 2020.

CONSTRUCTING COMMUNITY

The project became a testing ground for how the processes of designing and building could be incorporated into community-building. Working closely with GerHub we worked on the concept design, program, climatic response, and site selection. Strategically, we wanted to find a location where the idea of collective responsibility was already present. A key protagonist in that regard was Odgerel Gansukh, the owner of a garage door company in Songino Khairkhan-43. Odgerel, who has tales of finding human remains from the Stalinist purge of monks just behind his property, knows everyone in the district and is committed to improving life in his neighborhood. On the lot next door to his workshop is a place where he experiments. He has built a south-facing glazed winter garden with tomato plants, a mud brick stove, an unfinished concrete-block ger, and water retaining pond. His enthusiasm is infectious and he talks big plans, constantly digging, building, collecting, and inventing. Even if he can't always finish what he starts, he has succeeded in instilling a sense of identity into the area, which he calls EcoTown, and in building up a sense of collective ownership between residents. Odgerel was selected as the main contractor, and he sold a plot of land just below his workshop to GerHub. Working with him meant that we could plug into an existing network of established relationships, opening up communication channels with residents for us to increase awareness of what we were trying to achieve.

Throughout the design process, we maintained a deliberate position about our expertise as architects. Although we sought to engage residents and other stakeholders, the design was not participatory in the sense that the building was not designed by, or with, residents. Participatory design can often slip into models that are condescending and superficial, or that become a tick-box method when working in developing contexts. In some cases, a project's merit for its social purpose can come to override its architectural ambition. In such an approach, the social and the formal become irreconcilable.

Vernacular typologies offer an understanding of how the specific logics of a place can condition making and construction, but they should not be considered as replicable "truths." The fact that many have become obsolete is because of the various transitions that have occurred in their contexts.

This dilemma derives from the much-critiqued modernist position of the architect as problem-solver through formal invention. If the failures of the modernist project stem from the universality of its formal language applied ubiquitously to any and every context, the use of traditional vernacular forms or techniques of construction offers an approach towards local specificity. However, many of the contexts in which traditional forms evolved have so radically shifted through processes of global urbanization that the idea of returning to them as models is irrelevant. Vernacular typologies offer an understanding of how the specific logics of a place can condition making and construction, but they should not be considered as replicable 'truths.' The fact that many have become obsolete is because of the various transitions that have occurred in their contexts. These include changes to peoples' livelihoods, their access to information and knowledge of how people live elsewhere, their perspectives on their future and that of their children, and the demise of craft techniques and introduction of manufactured materials. In this regard, context is dynamic, subject to change, and replete with contradictions and conflicting agendas. Context is a plural condition, an 'assembly of things and agencies.'[111]

As architects, our intent is to engage with this expanded definition of context, to learn from the vernacular as an embodiment of the logics of place, yet to acknowledge that these logics have changed and thus that architecture and its material and constructive systems also must be rethought. This is the expertise and agency of the architect: not as an advocate of a singular formal language but rather as a spatial enabler, synthesizing a dialogue between the formal and the social, and between the disciplinary context of architecture and the messy reality of any given place. Design can contribute and further the discipline of architecture and trigger social change in the locations in which it operates. The social and the formal are not mutually exclusive or incompatible. One should not dominate the other.

This position materialized in our design of the Ger Innovation Hub. The attitude was to create something strange yet familiar, something that belonged to the place yet was formally alien. In part, this was to reciprocate what was happening in the context of the ger districts, where the ger is displaced from the rural context it was designed for —a nomadic miscreant incompatible with the forces of urbanization around it. This productive tension between the building and its location informs the Hub's design, in which a distinct geometric object encapsulates the circular imprint of a ger. Inspired by the ger's layered structural and material system of wood, felt, and canvas, these two layers are pulled apart to create a room within a room. Like a matryoshka doll, one building nestles within the other. The inner space has a sunken circular space at its center and is enclosed by L-shaped mud-brick walls in a cruciform orthogonal geometry, with each of the four end-walls made of openable polycarbonate panels, which are also used for the ceiling of this inner room. That entire structure is then set within an outer envelope of polycarbonate. Timber trusses structure both of these envelopes, allowing light to filter through to the center to maximize solar heat gain and warm the thermal mass of the interior. The in-between space acts as a buffer to trap radiant heat and to mediate the extreme differences in temperature between the interior and the exterior. In winter, this outer space is warmer than the outside, allowing kids to play and plants to grow. According to our initial environmental modelling, when the average daytime temperature is -21°C (-5.8°F), the inner room would be 18°C (64.4°F) warmer at -3°C (26.6°F). This means that to achieve a target of 18°C (64.4°F) for comfort, the energy required to heat the room would only need to make up a differential of 21°C (69.8°F) rather than 39°C (102.2°F), resulting in a potential reduction in energy consumption of up to 50 percent during the winter.

The Jockey Club project launched in the summer of 2018. Forty Hong Kong students travelled to Ulaanbaatar and worked tirelessly with local carpenters, construction workers, and ger district volunteers to assemble the wooden trusses and raise the timber structure in just two weeks. The structure was up, but there were no walls and no external cladding. The project remained just this timber frame for several months. Despite this, GerHub held an open-air event on Children's Day on June 1, 2019, to raise awareness about the project in the community.

This is the expertise and agency of the architect: not as an advocate of a singular formal language but rather as a spatial enabler, synthesizing a dialogue between the formal and the social, and between the disciplinary context of architecture and the messy reality of any given place.

Children play in the buffer space in January 2020 when the external temperature is -23°C (-9.4°F).

On the same day, they invited 70 members of the Young President's Organization, a group of international CEOs of successful companies under the age of forty-five. As a result they successfully raised the remaining funds required to complete the building.

TECHNOLOGICAL CERTAINTY

If the building of the Ger Innovation Hub was envisaged as a prototype with the potential to be replicable in other ger district locations, its performance would have to be quantified, measured, and evidenced. This shift into quantitative analysis reflects the difficulty that architecture grapples with in proving its effectiveness. Although its capability to instigate change in a community remained intangible and subject to time, its technological performance was something that could be collected and analyzed.

Upon completion of the building in January 2020 we installed data loggers within the different layered zones of the building. The onslaught of COVID-19 just after we returned from this trip meant that the building could not be opened to the public. All of GerHub's planned activities to engage residents were stalled and indefinitely postponed. Despite this drawback for the social impact of the project, it provided an ideal scenario to measure thermal performance, as recorded temperatures were the direct result of the passive thermal strategies in the unoccupied and unheated building. The collected results and subsequent analysis proved that the layered structure was effective: the outer skin maximized solar gain, trapping heat, and the buffer zone regulated the temperature, stabilizing the temperature of the interior.[112] This performance data was useful for GerHub in shaping their future programming, including planning activities during the winter in the late afternoon and early evening to benefit from the daily heat gains and thereby reduce energy consumption and costs.

Therein lies the technological innovation of the project: the tectonic strategy of pulling layers apart to create a buffer zone within a translucent skin that operates as an effective passive environmental tool at a relatively low cost.[113] In this regard, it can be seen as prototypical. This method could be deployed to other building scenarios such as housing, schools, workplaces, or existing buildings. The creation of different layers with different temperatures provides opportunities to program the building according to those climate zones rather than physical room divisions. The strategy could also be deployed in other extreme climates by changing the material properties of each layer. In hot climates, for example, the inner thermal mass could be protected from heat gain by a wrapper that provides shade, keeping the inner room as cool as possible. It is this core diagrammatic concept that is replicable and adaptable, not the specific form or function of the building itself. Thus, the project has the potential to bring about prototypical change, as opposed to typological transformation. The prototyping process here led to innovation with respect to the organization of space through a series of layered envelopes that can be applied to numerous building types or climatic conditions. It is a replicable spatial strategy; however, the process has not led to the evolution of a building type.

AN ECOLOGY OF PRACTICE

As a method of working, the origination, design, and construction of the Ger Innovation Hub offers an alternative form of architectural practice. The project started without a client, without a brief, without money, and without a site. It emerged through what can be defined as an 'ecology of practice,' a term that originated from our discussions with Francesco Garutti while setting up the curatorial agenda for 'The Things Around Us,' an exhibition held at the Canadian Center of Architecture in 2021.[114] This model of working shifts the role of the architect into that of an enabler, creating agency for a network of different stakeholders through the act of design and building.

In previous research that investigated the future evolution of Hong Kong's border with the mainland, we defined context as a dynamic ecology, replete with multiple actors, conditions, inputs, and feedback loops.[115] In this project, the intention was to propose design strategies that harnessed and augmented the preexisting dynamics occurring within the specific conditions of such an ecology. In Ulaanbaatar, the process of design and construction generated a specific set of connections and mutual dependencies between actors that could also be defined as an ecology. In the same way, our design proposal both augmented these existing dynamics and became a mechanism to adapt, transform, and evolve the system towards new aims. In other words, through the contextually attuned act of designing and building we can begin to shape, influence, and create an ecology of practice. The resulting network of relations is a broad and diverse assembly of representatives that consists of both existing relationships that are strengthened through the project and outside actors that are introduced to provide new triggers for change—for example, the local resident and friend of Odgerel responsible for the fabrication of the mudbricks as compared to the involvement of the Hong Kong Jockey Club's Rural-Urban Design Project. In this conceptual framework, building is the essential component and driver of an extended system. The process of building is a method to construct an ecology, providing agency for stakeholders and initiating new relationships that create transformative change.

The project also established *incrementality* as intrinsic to working within an ecology of practice. An incremental build-up of ideas shaped the project, from our initial tectonic experiments and field surveys to workshops and conversations with Badruun, Enkhjin, Dulguun, and Odgerel. These layers of information, assembled through a network of stakeholders, became the active ecology that functioned as an incubator of ideas—an environment where prototypes could develop, be tested, and sometimes get built.

The approach of incrementality was not preconceived as a linear process with a fixed goal or purpose, but rather emerged as a corollary to a series of events within the overall framework of the project. Most of these steps were nonsequential, however each one galvanized an intention that eventually coalesced in the construction of the building. This led us to consider whether incrementality could be instrumentalized within an ecology of practice.

This model of working shifts the role of the architect into that of an enabler, creating agency for a network of different stakeholders through the act of design and building.

The Ger Innovation Hub is a space that has enabled residents themselves to develop the collective identity of their neighborhood. It is also a prototype in the form of a multilayered structure that organizes space according to climatic zones. A scalable typology did not emerge here, but prototyping as a method, within the conception of both the context and the project as a dynamic ecology, set out a framework for continuing our work in Ulaanbaatar. The next step would be to incorporate incrementality as a strategy for structuring how the ger districts could develop over time.

The internal layer is opened up during a community workshop to discuss the future planning and activities of the Ger Innovation Hub, January 2020.

PLUG-IN: TRANSFORMING AND UPGRADING THE GER

At the heart of the unsustainable urbanization process in the ger districts is the ger itself. Its fast and affordable constructability—a positive for nomadic life on the steppe—is one of the main factors of the speed and extent of Ulaanbaatar's urban growth. The other main factor is the Second Land Law, which grants citizens the right to claim and own a plot of land. Passed in 2002, the law continues to propel the expansion of the city's territory. To alter the deleterious course of urbanization in the ger districts, either this policy would need to be superseded, or the ger must adapt into an urban typology that can support infrastructure and the creation of denser urban fabric. Because the ger is already integral to the lives of most ger district residents and remains the most pragmatic and affordable way to own a home, costing between $600 and $1,000, our aim is to transform this basic unit of habitation into a typology that can change how these settlements evolve to become more sustainable and liveable.

The ger is a nomadic typology. It is portable, easily disassembled and reassembled without any mechanical fixings. Its component parts are ready-mades that can be bought at everyday markets. The design has evolved out of the practicalities of limited material availability and life on the steppe. The lattice walls are made from thin laths of willow, slightly curved and jointed with soft leather that hardens over time, allowing the walls to expand and contract for ease of transportation. The crown and posts crafted from bent hardwood provide structural support for the wooden roof poles, which connect to the outer lattice walls. Felt—made from wool that has been beaten, washed, rolled, dried, and pressed until compact—is laid on top of the roof poles and outside of the lattice walls to provide insulation. White canvas wraps the exterior, providing water protection, and horsehair ropes tension the entire structure, stiffening it and providing its integral strength. Its circular form and low angled roof deflect wind. The door is always positioned to the south to minimise the cold from northerly winds.

When displaced to the city, this structure designed for mobility is paradoxically fixed within a rectangular plot contained by a two-meter-high fence (6.6 foot). In this context the ger is an unsuitable dwelling to support the needs of sedentary urban living. This is evident in its material performance. As a nomadic structure its constant movement through cycles of assembly and disassembly allows the felt insulation to breathe and the wood to remain dry. When immobile, however, it retains moisture, so the wood rots and the felt loses its insulative capabilities. Many residents we have spoken to have pointed to the difficulty of maintaining a ger in the city as a reason for why they were keen to move into a more permanent home.

In the city, the ger's trapped in this little fence. And who has time to take apart a perfectly fine ger and put it back up in exactly the same place? Because that doesn't happen, the ger rots and dilapidates easily. It doesn't breathe and get any air. A ger in the city isn't suitable. A house or apartment is better. It's much more comfortable.

Oyunbat

Urbanistically, the ger is also problematic. Its circular form is contained and introverted; the ger is an autonomous object, neither connected to nor reliant on any other structures or systems. Its interior encloses the life of the family within, separating domestic space from the commonality of the city outside. In contrast with the open steppe, in the ger districts the ger sits as an island-object within a bounded lot adjacent to a dirt road. There is no hierarchy of spaces between the public and private, no pavement or driveway, and no distinction between front and back. Such spatial organization is a (sub)urban concept very different from the traditional nomadic spatial relationship between the ger and the open expanse of the steppe. Yet, despite the various drawbacks of the ger as an urban typology, it remains the most economical form of dwelling. This somewhat obstinate staying power of the ger underscores the need to work with the typology itself in order to viably influence the pattern of growth in the ger districts.

To contextualize the current urbanization process in the ger districts from the perspective of residents, between 2019 and 2020 we conducted household surveys of living conditions and financial means in three separate districts, each a different type in respect to its proximity to the city center: urban, the closest to the citycenter, oldest and most dense with smaller plot sizes; mid, consolidated plots with road access; and fringe, farthest from city with larger plot sizes and often the most recent migrants.[116] The majority of fringe-district residents lived in a ger, there was an even split between gers and houses in the mid area, and more urban-district residents lived in houses.[117] This reflects that the longer people live in the ger districts, the more likely they are to build a house. Indeed, in our surveys, of those who had been living in the ger districts for more than twenty-one years,

80 percent lived in a house. However, we found that household income did not correlate similarly to housing type. Almost half of the high-income earners lived in a ger, and likewise half of the low-income earners had built a house.[118] When residents build a house they typically retain a ger on their plot for additional family members, storage, or as a summer kitchen. In one of our sample districts, Songino Khairkhan-43, 42 percent of the plots containing houses still contained one or more gers.

In our interviews we also found that 95 percent of residents were dissatisfied with their current dwelling. One option available to them would be to sell their land and move to an apartment in the city with central heating and sanitation infrastructure. However, the cost of an apartment remains out of reach for many residents due to the low value of their ger district land, their monthly income, and their current debt.[119] Additionally, 63 percent of residents surveyed were reluctant to give up their land and preferred to improve their living conditions on their own plot. When improvements are made, most do so incrementally according to their financial ability. Some residents initially modify their ger by adding a simple wooden threshold to prevent heat loss or by building permanent concrete foundations to limit the cold coming from the ground. Over time, more than 65 percent of families' self-build a baishin, the common simple house.[120] Typically, the baishin also progresses in stages during summer construction seasons, with the foundation, walls, roof, and then interior fit-out taking up to three years to complete. Compared to the ger, however, most of these houses offer no improvement to infrastructure or thermal comfort.[121] According to a 2018 study by the Mongolian University of Science and Technology, the average thickness of insulation in 93 percent of houses in the ger districts falls well below the minimum standards for energy efficiency.[122] Compounding this issue is the widespread use of inefficient wood or coal-burning stoves for heating, resulting in more fuel being consumed.[123] In fact, in our household surveys we found that on average a baishin consumes more coal for heating than a ger, primarily due to the increased area of the houses and their greater rates of heat loss.[124]

Our fieldwork and research has established criteria for evaluating dwelling prototypes in the ger districts and developing new ones. Neither the ger or the baishin can structure the districts towards the creation of more sustainable urban fabric, due to their energy inefficiency, lack of infrastructure, and inability to densify. A prototype therefore needs to offer an alternative model that can address these issues, but beyond that it must also be affordable and comparable to the cost of a standard baishin.[125] Given that many residents still use a ger even when they have built a house, the prototype should integrate the ger into the dwelling to conform with how people already live. Additionally, in accordance with how residents phase the construction of their houses based on affordability, the concept of incrementality can be deployed not only to structure sequential growth of the building but also to consider how the districts can increase in density over time—incrementality being key method of our approach to begin to galvanise a community into action. For us, incrementality is both strategic, as a mechanism to initiate the networked activity of an ecology of practice, and also highly pragmatic, based simply on what people can afford.

For us, incrementality is both strategic, as a mechanism to initiate the networked activity of an ecology of practice, and also highly pragmatic, based simply on what people can afford.

THE STORY
Zul-Erdene Sharavjamts & Urangua Shagdar

Excerpts from *Ger District Portraits*, presented at the
Venice Biennale 2016, produced by filmmaker Dulguun
Bayasgalan.

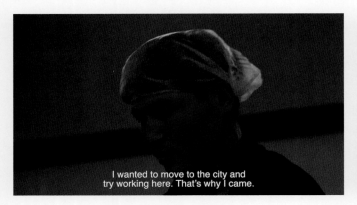

I wanted to move to the city and try working here. That's why I came.

Our goals for the next three years are to have a nice house...

...and start a nice family.

But first we need to make our own lives better...

THE PROTOTYPE: GER PLUG-IN 1.0
The tectonic explorations we had undertaken at the at the Venice Biennale 2016 were predecessors of an idea to create a hybrid between a traditional ger and a house, linking vernacular and contemporary construction systems together. The idea, which became known as the Ger Plug-In, was to provide the ger with everything that it doesn't currently have in infrastructural terms but also to integrate it into a permanent structure. In March 2016 I proposed the Plug-In project to Pierre Lorinet, who was active in sponsoring social and educational projects in Mongolia and had reached out to me after an article in the Financial Times in January 2015.[126] He backed the idea with a donation to the University of Hong Kong to design and realize the project.

The first step was to test the timber structure of the prototype by organizing a design-build workshop with students from the University of Hong Kong and vocational training students from the Institute of Engineering and Technology, Ulaanbaatar (IET), a contact Badruun had

Otherwise, it's hard to raise a kid in such a small ger.

We don't want to ask for anything from our parents.

We at least want a bigger ger before we have any children.

We want to have our own family built with our own hands.

put us in touch with. IET provided a classroom, wood workshop, and a yard where we could construct the timber structure. With our work set out to resolve the geometry and assembly details of the structure, we were designing right up to the last moment on the plane. Nevertheless, the efforts of the entire team enabled the structure of the first Plug-In to be constructed. This first test only resolved issues of the structure, and so we spent the next six months resolving the integration of infrastructure, thermal performance, wall surfaces, and exterior cladding. Retaining the idea of splicing the traditional structure of the ger with timber construction, we grafted the ger to a timber-frame building to create a hybrid living space that is part ger, part new structure. A truss suspends the ger from above, allowing the central columns to be removed and the stove to be relocated within the thermal mass of a brick wall. The resulting open, obstruction-free space is safer and provides the family with more options for how to inhabit the room. The environmental performance of the house is improved with systems that include a septic treatment system

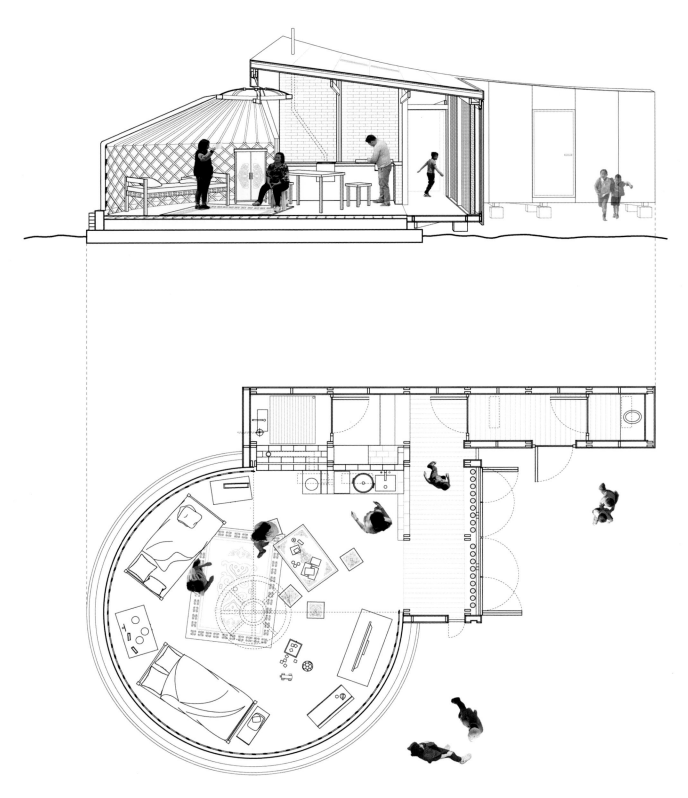

The first prototype: Ger Plug-In 1.0.

0m 1m 2m

and toilet, a water tank and shower, underfloor heating, an electric boiler, as well as thick insulation that wraps the entire structure. Furthermore, we oriented the glazing towards the south to benefit from solar gain and created a passive solar Trombe wall made of black PVC pipes filled with sand. This would heat up during the day and release the radiant heat back to the interior during the night.

The building systems were selected after a careful appraisal of available technologies and costs. For water supply, the only option other than truck delivery is to dig a well to reach the aquifer, which is unaffordable at a household scale, plus the water quality is suspect.[127] For the toilet system, we weighed the pros and cons of a flush system against those of a dry composting toilet. Because average temperatures fall below zero for six months of the year, composting toilets require additional engineering and heating, making this option impractical. Although water-based, the selected septic tank treats waste on site and provides excess treated water that can be used for irrigation. For energy supply, the costs of renewables such as photovoltaics are still too high for household application.[128] However, by increasing the thermal performance of the house, less energy is required for heating. By heating with electricity, which is produced in power stations away from populated areas, as opposed to a coal-burning stove, a significant reduction of local air pollution can be achieved. However, for the first test, we opted for a dual coal and electric stove to supply underfloor heating and a hot water radiator system, and to be used for cooking. Because the ger districts are prone to electrical outages, we did not want the residents to be out of heat for any length of time during the winter. We also wanted to monitor whether the inhabitants would shift away from coal use despite electricity incurring more monthly costs.

In May 2017 the detailed design was complete, and we were ready to commence construction of the Ger Plug-In 1.0. The project was conceptualised as a live experiment. A young couple who we had interviewed during our research for the 2016 Venice Biennale, Zulaa and Urangua, were willing to participate. In one of the films that Dulguun made for the exhibition, the couple had expressed their aspirations for a nice house where they could raise a family.

> Our goal for the next three years is to have a nice house, maybe a car, a couple of kids, and start a nice family. But first we need to make our own lives better, and make sure we're not deprived of anything before we bring a child. … It is hard to raise a kid in a small ger. A small ger isn't easy.
>
> Zul-Erdene Sharavjamts and Urangua Shagdar[129]

In exchange for the house, Zulaa and Urangua allowed us to build on their land and let us access the building to collect data. The Plug-In was completed in late August 2017, and the couple moved in at that time. Every month we asked them to provide their electric bills and to measure their water and coal consumption. Every three months we conducted an interview to ascertain changes to their living quality.

After living in the Ger Plug-In for one year, everyday life had changed for Zulaa and Urangua. Instead of having to walk thirty minutes to collect water every day, the couple now had access to a one-ton water tank refilled by a truck every seven to ten days. They showered three times a week in winter and every day in summer. They also shared the shower with other families in the district. During the winter of 2018, when the lowest recorded temperature was -39°C (-38.2°F), they were happy not to have to leave the house to use the toilet. They preferred to use electricity as their energy source rather than coal, and paid approximately the same amount on their electrical bill as a typical ger household.[130] This is most likely due to both the compact size and improved insulation of the Plug-In. They used 93 percent less coal than the average yearly consumption for a single ger, an estimated 0.27 tons compared to an average of 3.8 tons. This represents a potential savings of 871,000 tons of coal per year if each of the city's 246,800 ger households were to be replaced with a Ger Plug-In.[131]

To obtain precise temperature readings, six data loggers had been installed in the Plug-In at different locations, including the main living space, entry threshold, and oculus rooflight. We had also installed the same loggers in a traditional ger to provide a baseline to measure the Plug-In against. In the first year of testing, we recorded that when the external temperature was between -10°C (14°F) and -20°C (-4°F), the Plug-In was 2.5°C (36.5°F) warmer than the traditional ger. The Plug-In also was more thermally stable than the ger, fluctuating by 4°C (39.2°F) compared to 10°C (50°F). With the additional thermal mass of the Plug-In, during a period of inoccupation when the exterior temperatures ranged from -23 to 12.5°C (-9.4 to 53.6°F), it took five days for all parts of the interior to fall to negative temperatures.

The initial period of data collection provided us with evidence that the Ger Plug-In prototype succeeded in providing better access to sanitation, reducing heat loss, and significantly reducing coal consumption relative to a traditional ger. This empirical method of evaluation represented an extension of our practice as architects, as we equipped ourselves with measuring devices and became adept in recording and analysing data. This was necessary to prove that the Ger Plug-In worked from a technological perspective, but was it affordable? The Plug-In pilot cost around $13,000, which falls within the $8,000–20,000 cost range of a standard baishin. However, many residents phase the building of their houses, so such upfront costs could remain out of reach for many. Could we make the project more affordable yet maintain its environmental performance? And crucially, if these economic demands were met, would residents prefer a Plug-In to a standard house?

In addition to considering those factors that concerned the awareness and buy-in of ger district residents, in developing the pilot into a scalable product we would also come to engage with banks and their financial instruments. Since 2018, the Green Climate Fund (GCF), which was set up by the United Nations Framework Convention on Climate Change (UNFCCC), has been supporting the development of new eco-banking financial products in the housing sector. In October 2018 we met with the Mongolian Sustainable Finance Association, a group of Mongolian banks formed to assist and implement procedures for green finance opportunities.[132] This program, underwritten by the GCF and the Mongolian government, resulted in certain local banks being able to create mortgage products with improved loan rates, 8–12 percent compared to 18 percent, for housing that met the criteria of a 20 percent improvement to the thermal performance stipulated by the Mongolian regulations.[133] To assist in setting up a standardized mechanism to evaluate housing products and connect construction companies to these loans, the Energy Efficient Project was launched in 2020 by the Deutsche Gesellschaft für Internationale Zusammenarbeit (GIZ), a German federally owned development agency. Under the process established, construction drawings are sent to GIZ to be audited based on material U-values and overall volume of the building. If the 20 percent improvement is met, the housing product is given an energy efficient certificate, which then enables customers to apply for one of the green mortgage loans.

Currently, fourteen different companies with different housing products have been taken up by the scheme, each using a different system of construction, and five have been built on the grounds of a kindergarten in Songino Khairkhan district as a showcase for people to view and to learn more about financing options.[134] To kickstart the scheme, GIZ offered a 30 percent subsidy to the first fifty customers taking out a loan. Unfortunately, take-up of the project was very low: only twenty-five of these houses were built between 2020 and 2022.[135] The most likely reason for this is affordability. The lowest mortgage interest rate in 2021 was offered by Golomt Bank at just over 6 percent and requiring a minimum deposit of 10 percent. This equates to a minimum $2,072 down payment and monthly paybacks of $159. Given that the average monthly income is $421, the mortgage is still out of reach for many residents. Most ger district residents are used to borrowing money in the form of short-term loans, but not in the form of mortgages.[136]

In comparison, the Ger Plug-In 1.0 prototype provides more space for less cost—$245 per square meter (per 10,8 square foot) compared to $430–$650 per square meter (per 10,8 square foot) for the other approved house models—without compromising on performance. The pilot project has been inhabited since 2017, a live experiment whereby qualitative and quantitative data can be constantly collected and updated. However, to qualify for the green loans, the Plug-In would have to be independently audited by GIZ to obtain the Energy Efficient Construction Certificate. If successful, this would allow thousands of ger district residents access to these loans, potentially proliferating the Plug-In as an alternative housing typology.

ITERATIVE DESIGN: GER PLUG-IN 2.0 TO 3.0

The pilot project exposed two main areas in need of improvement. Firstly, because it involved removing one quarter of the ger's wall panels it led to heat losses at the interface between the ger and the new structure. This was pointed out to us by Tuvshinkhuu Samdan, an engineer at GIZ, who conducted thermal image analysis of the Plug-In to locate areas of heat loss. Secondly, the feedback on the financial practicalities of constructing the building in one go led us to divide the structure into two components that could be constructed in phases. The new design, Ger Plug-In 2.0, consists of a ger connected to a core component—containing a toilet, shower, kitchen unit, and heating system—and a secondary component designed as an extension that houses living and sleeping spaces. The infrastructural core is twelve square meters and the extension is twenty-five. Added to an existing ger of 26 square meters (279.9 square foot), the first phase house is thus a total of 38 square meters (409 square foot) and the extended house sixty-three. This design takes advantage of the ger as the ready-made, cheapest way to build a dwelling in the ger districts. The idea is that residents can purchase the core unit at a relatively low price and then extend it when they need and are financially able to do so. This aligns with the form of incremental building that we know is the prevalent model in the districts.

Based on feedback from engineers at GIZ and our contractor in Ulaanbaatar, we relooked at the design's material build-up and construction details to improve thermal performance. This back-and-forth and subsequent finalisation of the details led to the successful certification of the Ger Plug-In 2.0 as an energy efficient dwelling in September 2021, making it eligible for the low-interest mortgages. Throughout our discussions with GIZ they have responded positively to the design as they recognize that it will be the only certified housing product that integrates a ger and thus will fill a gap in the market due to its lower costs.

We decided to test this by undertaking another set of surveys to ascertain the market potential of version 2.0. It took 178 interviews in order to hit a target of 50 positive responses, meaning households that want to buy the Plug-In and are in a financial position to do so, representing a positive response rate of 28 percent. These households have no overdue or non-performing loans, possess ownership of their land, have an average monthly income of over ₮800,000 ($280) per month, meet the 45 percent debt-to-income ratio requirement of the banks, and therefore can afford the Ger Plug-In 2.0. If we extrapolate this proportion across the 246,800 ger district households, this equates to an estimated 69,000 households who would be interested in the Plug-In, giving it a market potential of over $749 million, based on a unit cost of $10,849. With this information the project again shifted, this time to think of the Ger Plug-In as an opportunity to create a sustainable enterprise.

However, when we discussed our design with the banks, they were concerned with the implications of including what they considered a movable structure within a mortgage product. Even though we argued that in our design the ger had become permanent due to its integral connection with the house, they remained reticent. Some residents also pushed back against our design's inclusion of a ger. As Songino Khairkhan resident Sanchir Batbold told us, *"It is a lot of work. Rainwater cladding is really important when we think about maintenance. We are not living in a ger out of choice."*[137]

The Ger Plug-In built prototype, August 2017.

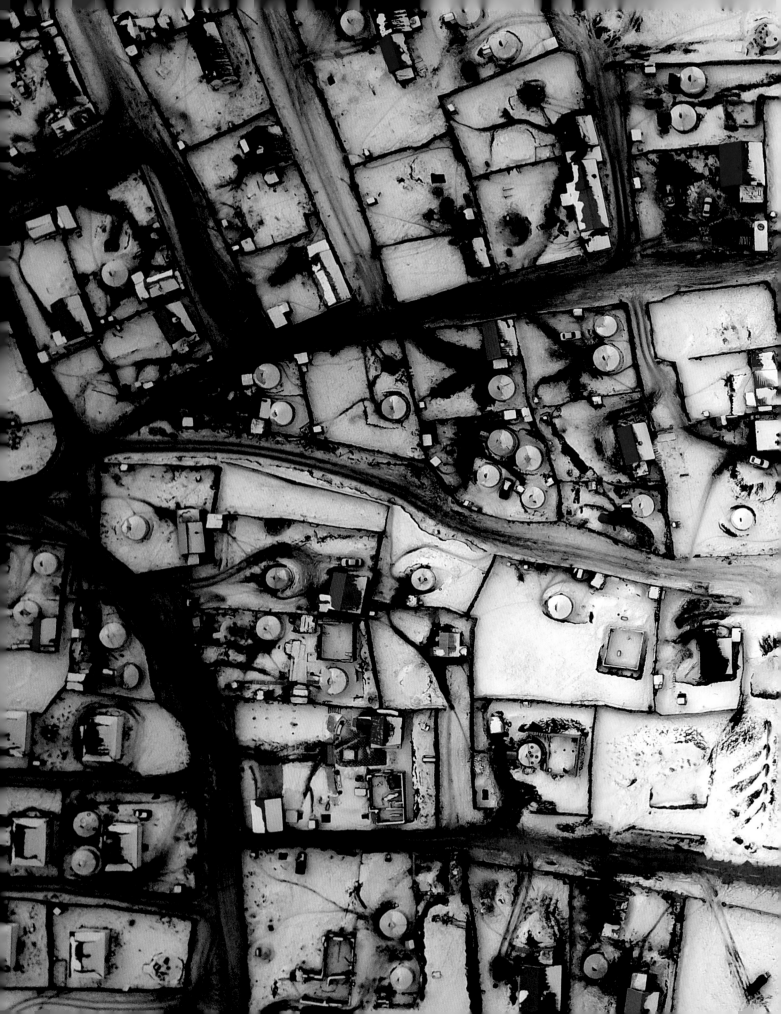

The Ger Plug-In is located on the edge of Bayankhoshuu district, December 2017.

Given that the success of the prototype would be dependent on residents' ability to access finance, we could not risk our product being unmortgageable, and so we developed Ger Plug-In 3.0. In this version we separated the design into three distinct parts: the connector, the core, and the extension. This allows the core and extension to be independently mortgaged as permanent structures separate from the ger and the connector. It also allows the financing to be broken into smaller and more affordable tranches. In some ways it represents a conceptual inversion of our original logic. The ger does not incrementally become a house, but rather the house has the possibility of attaching a ger.

By thinking about the design in this way, the connector becomes a critical piece that could be applied to any house, whether a different prototype of ours or an existing building. The connector is a universal port, built according to the ger's geometry and dimensions yet adaptable to attach to different opening sizes. As a minimal intervention at the lowest price, the connector offers the relocation of the stove, the removal of the central columns, a threshold to prevent heat loss, and increased thermal insulation for the ger. And although this piece will not be eligible for the subsidized mortgage program, it does open other funding streams such as Eco Consumption Loans for heating or insulation retrofits.

The separation of the design in version 3.0 into distinct phases and components allows residents to choose a housing provision best suited to their needs and their income. It creates the possibility to integrate the ger or not to have one at all. The phasing of components harnesses the incremental and self-build culture that exists in the ger districts, allowing families to adapt as they see fit. However, the impact of COVID-19 and consequent closure of the Chinese border, with only intermittent reopening, since February 2020 resulted in supply-chain blockages and escalating costs of materials. The cost of timber, for example, went up by approximately 70 percent from 2018 to 2021.[138] This meant that the estimated cost of the Plug-In increased from $10,849 in 2018 to $23,860 in 2021. To reflect this change in operations and costs, we adapted the design to minimize any materials that could not be locally sourced, exchanging the preferred timber frame with more readily available concrete blocks for an update on version 3.0. This meant that our intention to set up timber prefabrication had to pause as it was no longer economically viable given that supplies of timber were much reduced. It also meant requalifying version 3.0 with GIZ to make sure the new material build-up still met the criteria for energy efficiency. The inability to travel from Hong Kong to Mongolia since 2020 also impacted how quickly we could move the project forward. As well as modifying the detailed design, we used the time to develop the idea of using the project to create a sustainable enterprise.

EXPANDING AN ECOLOGY OF PRACTICE
Our role as architect expanded to that of entrepreneur as we initiated an architectural start-up to apply our knowledge of tested prototypes to develop scalable, marketable products. The intent with the start-up is to create an agency that can set up local partnerships in Ulaanbaatar to build

Ger Plug-Ins in the ger districts. Any revenue generated is fed back into the business to further develop new prototypes or improve existing products. In 2020 we incorporated this start-up, called District Development Unit, as a spin-off of our research lab at the University of Hong Kong. Based on our predicted revenues and market research the demand in the first year was projected to be 1,125 units, representing a total income of over $12 million and a profit potential of $2.07 million, based on a margin of 17 percent. Although we could not anticipate meeting this demand in our first year of operation it signified the potential of the business. This was recognized by an investor in Hong Kong who was interested in helping to set up the company in Mongolia by offering financial and marketing support, albeit as a majority stakeholder. However, the economic slide and increased inflation caused by COVID-19 hit ger district residents hard in 2021, with monthly incomes dropping by 4 percent while costs for construction materials rose by approximately 52 - 92 percent.[139] This gap in affordability meant that the profit margin of our business venture was not guaranteed, and the investor backed out until the conditions changed. However, this proved fortuitous in some respects as we decided to press on with the formation of the company as a local implementation unit, partnering with our long-term contractor and another collaborator with expertise in business management. This preserved our equity in this newly formed company, named Energy Efficient Design and Build (Энержи эфишент дизайн бюлд), and allowed us, during the winter of 2021, to prepare for the summer construction season and to launch our product. As we move forward, the gap between affordability and the construction costs of our desired thermal performance remains the most difficult bridge to cross, and we have yet to determine whether our product can still be attractive to residents as we gradually return to a post-Covid, or with-Covid, future.

Overall, the Ger Plug-In 3.0 offers more space for less money compared to the other energy efficient housing products on the market. It is also the only product that is extendible, offering a possibility of incremental staging and growth according to residents' financial capacity. It is also strategically agile, already proving its ability to adapt to different construction systems in response to price increases, or to the lack of imported materials due to pandemic-related border closures. We initially assumed that factory production would streamline efficiency and reduce costs. However, given the current uncertainty of global supply chains and the fragility of the Mongolian economy, the present approach is to stay small, training local construction teams and sub-contractors to implement orders. This process is ongoing, involving a constant back-and-forth in the attempt close the gap between affordability and performance. If, in the next stages of development, we can assist residents in accessing low-interest eco-loans, many households will be able to obtain sustainable housing and remain on their plot.

Though the initial pilot took just fourteen months from design to completion, it has taken five years and three versions to evolve the design from a pilot to a scalable product. The process has revealed that getting to the point at which architecture can be considered a product requires an expansion of the role of the architect. Historically, many architects have attempted to do this, including Jean Prouvé, Le Corbusier, Walter Gropius, Frank Lloyd Wright, and Buckminster Fuller.[140] However, all of their business ventures failed. Today, there is enthusiasm around digital manufacturing techniques and a resurgence in the idea of factory-produced homes, but the majority of these are designed as universal models, applicable to any site or location. Some, offered by global brands like Muji and Ikea, offer the lifestyle choices of minimal aesthetics and dwelling sizes that nevertheless are priced between $2,000 and $4,000 per square meter (per 10.8 square foot).[141]

The difference in our approach is as follows. The design is rooted locally. It originates from an understanding of the specific characteristics of place in terms of climate, finance, and social constraints. It harnesses existing processes of transformation such as incremental improvement to augment and evolve an existing typology. Additionally, our method to create typological change through an ecology of practice is different. First, to prove that the building was sustainable we measured its performance empirically and had it certified by an independent auditor. Second, we conducted fieldwork to obtain evidence that residents could afford it and that they would be interested in purchasing it. Third, we were entrepreneurial in considering financial strategies, legal agreements, and company structures that would enable this new housing typology to be constructed across the ger districts at scale. To do this, we had to become adept at talking to banks and investors and to consider the project from their perspective. In turn, we had to think creatively when their financial mechanisms were too rigid or remained out of reach for many ger district residents, as when we modularised the components of the Plug-In so that they could be more affordable or funded through other types of loans.

In the effort to address the untenable effects of the current mode of urbanization in the ger districts, the Ger Plug-In is the only housing model available that integrates the traditional ger with new construction. The Ger Plug-In breaks the ger's formal autonomy by attaching an orthogonal dwelling to its circular geometry. The ger becomes conjoined to a linear structure that enables the dwelling to adhere to the plot boundary. This alignment of the house to the fence wall allows the structure to negotiate with its external environment, whether that is an adjacent plot, the street, or a residual public space. This negotiation of the edge and how it relates to its context signifies the ger's transformation from a nomadic typology to the Plug-In, an urban typology with the capacity to construct a new urban fabric. It represents a potential new typology and building block of the city that is rooted in tradition yet is positioned strategically for the future.

This negotiation of the edge and how it relates to its context signifies the ger's transformation from a nomadic typology to the Plug-In, an urban typology with the capacity to construct a new urban fabric.

The splice between the traditional ger and the contemporary house, May 2022.

View of the Ger Plug-In looking back
towards Thermal Power Plant No. 4
and the city center, August 2017.

So, about the three neighbors north of my khashaa. The four of us are very well connected and cooperative together. We help each other to get things from the shop, or by taking their water containers in our car when we go to the water kiosk. So, in this way, we are very close. Even our children play together, and they look after each other. This is also very comforting for us when they all get along. Personally, I am closer to my neighbors than my in-laws who live on the other side of my plot.

Sanchir Batbold

INCRE

UR

STRA

MENTAL
BAN
TEGY

Visiting households to understand
the diversity of needs and incomes
in the ger districts, January 2020.

INCREMENTAL URBAN STRATEGY

Under the current model, planning of the ger districts is done almost entirely under the auspices of the Asian Development Bank (ADB). The ADB conceives and initiates redevelopment plans through collaborations with government bureaus, international consultants, and local partners. Following the approval of such projects in the Mongolian parliament, the ADB provides preferential loans to the government and assists with project implementation and coordination of different specialist consultant teams. The present, ADB-backed strategy for ger district development is to create four subcenters, with connections to high-speed bus routes and new infrastructure to support densification in the form of five- and six-story townhouses.[142] The intention is to stimulate the housing market and assist developers by preparing the land for development. This includes confirming land exchange agreements with landowners, funding infrastructure, and negotiating preferential mortgage rates for consumers.

The ADB plan to improve housing is contingent on residents voluntarily exchanging their 500 to 700 square meter (5382 to 7534.7 square foot) plots of land for 37 to 42 square meter (398 to 452 square foot) apartments. Economic recession has meant income levels of ger districts are low—on average ₮1,157,500 ($406) per month[143]—while promised 'low-interest' mortgages for the housing are much higher than expected, at between 8 percent and 16.8 percent. This means that the success of the market-rate housing component of the ADB scheme is uncertain, which has put off developers. Even if successful, the tracts of housing currently planned for development at the Bayankhoshuu, Selbe, Dambadarjaa, and Denjiin subcenters will only provide capacity for approximately 12 percent of the total ger district population of 840,000.[144] Based on our research, we estimate that 63 percent of that population wish to improve their housing whilst remaining on their existing *khashaa,* or plot.[145] That suggests there is an urgent need for an alternative development strategy that can work for all ger district residents (not just those in selected areas), that allows residents to stay on their own plots, and that is not reliant on developer or government funding.

The Ger Plug-In is an attempt to initiate such an alternative urban model to the ADP subcenters master plan. Its fundamental idea is to set out a mechanism for the ger to adapt from a nomadic to an urban typology. However, one size does not fit all. As our fieldwork and household surveys evidenced, ger district residents have a diversity of needs and incomes. Furthermore, for those plots that already have a house, which represented 69 percent of all households in our 2019 survey,[146] the Plug-In can only offer an additional dwelling for relatives or a rental unit for new migrants. It cannot improve the provision of infrastructure to the plot or the thermal performance of existing structures. Although the Plug-In itself is designed to be built incrementally, its potential to increase density in the ger districts is limited to its repetition, by adding more units to each plot.

Rather than rubberstamp it as a singular typology across the districts, our aim is to include the Plug-In within a strategy that diversifies dwelling types, increases density, and provides infrastructure that can expand as the population increases.

Rather than rubberstamp it as a singular typology across the districts, our aim is to include the Plug-In within a strategy that diversifies dwelling types, increases density, and provides infrastructure that can expand as the population increases. Implementing such a strategy could improve the overall sustainability of the city and offer an alternative to the current pattern of sprawl and outward expansion. To realize such an alternative necessitates thinking beyond individual land parcels and considering what can be shared as collective resources at which scales. Our approach is to build up a set of ingredients that can create beneficial mechanisms of collaboration at different scales, rather than through a top-down master plan.

FOUR-PLOT

To develop models of such shared cooperation that would be accessible for all residents, we have used a base unit of four adjacent plots. This was chosen as an appropriate scale because two plots would be a binary with a risk of oppositional views between neighbors while four require negotiation between households from different kinship networks. A four-plot condition also can be considered as the structuring unit of the ger-districts settlement. It is typically positioned between two parallel roads and repeats horizontally until meeting a perpendicular road. The fence wall between adjacent plots and the boundary to a road are thus the two fundamental edge conditions structuring ger district growth. Three such four-plot clusters were selected as sites for our design research, each representing a different, yet typical, state of transformation occurring in the settlement. The strategies developed for each sample could therefore be extended and applied to similar conditions found throughout the districts. The aim was to demonstrate how four households could improve not only their individual dwellings but also their collective land plots, including opportunities for shared resources such as water, waste, and potentially heat and power.

The three clusters are in Songino Khairkhan-43, the same district in which the Ger Innovation Hub is located. Strategically, it made sense to reinforce the active network of stakeholders that had been initiated through that project. The criteria for selecting plots were two-fold. First, the plots had to correspond with different stages of transformation that had been identified in our analysis, each with distinct spatial characteristics.[147] Second, residents had to be willing to assist in data collection and engage in workshops. The Khoroo governor and kheseg leaders helped identify the most appropriate residents. Based on their input and interviews with families the three clusters were selected.

The first cluster is located at the very edge of the urban settlement, its residents establishing their plots within the last 5 to 10 years. It has an irregular plot boundary, and only one road runs parallel to the plots. There are four gers, one completed house, and one house under construction. Demographically this cluster represents young families. When we first met the residents in 2019, eight adults were under twenty-five, all nine children were under the age of eleven, and just one grandparent was over sixty. The second cluster is more established, with one household claiming their khashaa over twenty years ago and a total of three houses already built. The plots are arranged two-by-two on sloped terrain between two parallel roads, the lower plots located conveniently adjacent to a water kiosk. This cluster is extreme in the nature of the household structures. In one plot, thirteen people live in just two gers, while in another a retired grandmother lives in a house by herself. The third cluster has plots arranged side-by-side in a linear strip between two roads. The residents here established their plots ten to fifteen years ago. The average income is slightly higher than the other clusters and the residents are slightly older, with six out of fifteen adults over the age of fifty.

Based on household interviews there is a big range of financial capacities within each cluster. Some families are comfortable taking out loans to develop additional investment properties and businesses on their plots whilst others are unemployed and completely reliant on government financial support. The plots contain different generations, ages, and numbers of family members. For the most part, cooperation between neighbors is already common practice. Residents described how neighbors would assist in shopping if they were going to the market, offer car rides to the bus stop, or look after children, while common areas were set out for tree planting and collective play spaces. This indicates the potential for sharing resources and undertaking improvement works together as a community cluster, although currently all upgrading is undertaken only by each individual household and construction is incremental and based on available finances.

CATALOGUE OF COMPONENTS
The clusters represent a cross-section of the spatial conditions, economic conditions, and household structures found in the ger districts. A singular housing typology is not effective in meeting their diverse requirements. Instead, using design logics from the specificities of each cluster, we created a series of prototypes of housing and infrastructural upgrades that could be applied to the districts at large.

Ger Plug-In Core

Ger Plug-In Extended

Ger Plug-In without ger

*A ger is
a lot of work and
commitment. We are trying
to move away from it. Is it
foreign fascination that they
want to keep it? Do they know
how hard it is to keep and
maintain a ger?*

Oyunseren Tsevel

Ger Plug-In Series

Erdenchimeg, thirty-three, lives with her husband and five children in a ger. She is unemployed and receives child welfare benefits from the government. Erdenchimeg shares a plot with her sister and family. Currently, three generations and thirteen people live in just two gers. Her situation is representative of the poorest residents in the districts. The incremental design of the Ger Plug-In series of components allows the family to improve their living conditions gradually. The most affordable first step is to install the Ger Connector to the door of the existing ger, creating a new threshold. Throughout the ger districts one can find many examples of simple wooden structures self-built by residents to prevent heat loss. Based on these, the Connector design also includes retrofitting the ger with new insulation and a steel structure that allows the central columns to be removed to create an obstacle-free space. This connector can then be used to attach to the Plug-In's Core module, which provides infrastructure including a shower, toilet, kitchen, and electrical heating. Over time, this can be further extended into a house. In each stage of expansion, window and door elements are reused to prevent waste and to minimize expense.

However, some residents felt strongly that they did not want to live in a ger anymore. For these households, an alternative is to directly invest in the Extension component of the Plug-In, omitting the ger entirely. In the future, if their needs change, they could add the connector and ger as an additional space. The negative feedback regarding the ger changed our thinking and indicated the necessity to create housing models with the flexibility to add a ger, as opposed to gradually transitioning from a ger to a house. However, both routes are open as possibilities depending on the different needs and financial constraints of the residents.

Apartment House

Our research pointed to the need for a house with infrastructure that could allow for flexible arrangements of inhabitation, given the various multi-generational family structures found on each plot. This is due to the fact that many relatives live in the same or adjacent plots when first moving to the city. For example, Idersaikhan, thirty-two, lives together with his wife, three young children, and mother in the winter, but in warmer months they separate into two gers. The Apartment House has three arms in a trident form with a central infrastructural core. A ger can be attached to each arm to provide additional accommodation. This allows for multiple forms of occupation. Different generations of the same family can share the infrastructure of a bathroom and kitchen as well a large communal space for dining, living, and working while maintaining their own sleeping spaces by attaching individual gers to the main body of the house. This arrangement would be helpful for intergenerational families such as that of Oyunchimeg Dunkher. She lives in a plot next to three of her children who have families of their own. She has seven grandchildren, five of them under the age of 10, and it has become her job to look after them when their parents are working. Effectively, her current house often becomes a playroom. The Apartment House would provide Oyunchimeg with a common space that could be used as a play space, yet allow each family to sleep in their own ger. It would also offer her the potential to earn additional income by looking after other neighborhood children—on the other side of the road live another ten children under the age of ten.

Apartment House without Ger

The Apartment House can also accommodate different, unrelated households. The house can be split into a maximum of three separate units, each with its own bathroom, kitchen, living space, and ger. The infrastructure shares the same septic tank, drainage, and water inlet pipes, reducing the outlay for each family. Alternatively, a family could live in two wings of the Apartment House and rent out the third unit to another family, providing a regular source of monthly income. It is further possible to link two Apartment Houses laterally, the two conjoined arms forming a large space suitable for commercial programs. A household could then sell or lease the units, a desire expressed by some of the higher earning families. Furthermore, linking to Apartment Houses allows the system to increase density on each plot.

Apartment House with Ger

Apartment House Double with Gers

Half House and Infrastructural Core

All the selected four-plot sites contained households that had either already built a house or commenced the construction of one. However, these houses lack water or septic tanks and sufficient insulation. For those at an initial stage of construction, a model is needed to complete their build to include better insulation and infrastructure. Munkhdalai and Chantsaldulam, who have five children, built a concrete foundation with block walls in 2018. They are like many who incrementally build a house, adding elements each summer based on what they can afford. The Half-House typology comprises an additional trussroof and infrastructural module that can complete the house and provide sanitation and improved thermal performance. A pitched roof affords a loft space for sleeping, and the house can connect to an existing ger in anticipation of children requiring more space as they get older. If a house has been completed, as on the plot of Gunbat and Oyunseren, a Core Infrastructure module can be added at the main door, serving as a thermal threshold and providing a toilet, shower, water tank, and hot water boiler.

Half House

Landscape Infrastructure

The housing prototypes comprising our catalogue of component address the needs of the residents at the building scale. The accompanying step was to strategize how to situate these buildings on site and how to provide and extend infrastructure to meet demand without undue costs for residents. There are many obstacles to shared infrastructure, including the need to demarcate plots with fences to prove legal ownership, and a reluctance to share waste and water provision between plots with different needs.

Infrastructure Core

However, there are clear operational and economic advantages to sharing. The sizing and type of infrastructural upgrades for the four-plot clusters were calculated by monitoring residents' consumption of water, electricity,

All my life I have lived in a ger and only in the last decade or so, I have lived in a baishin. I struggled and struggled to reach this life. Wow! All my kids have grown up with their own families and are living comfortably. I worked very hard to raise my kids alone, but now, all is good.

Oyunchimeg Dunkher

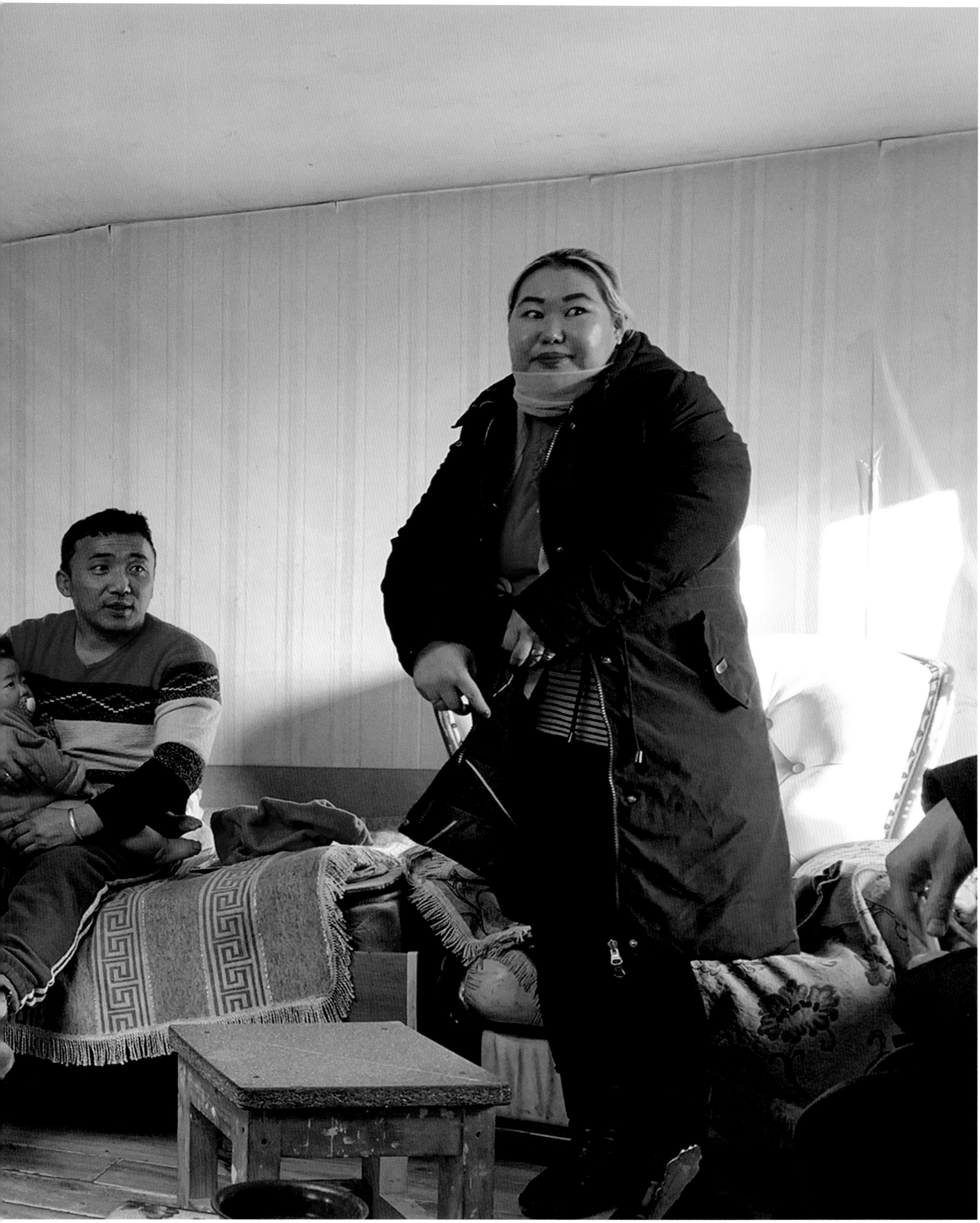

and fuel,[148] and then projecting that data onto the future density target prescribed by the ADB which is 3.6 times the number of households on each plot.[149] In the case of Cluster 1 this would mean an increase from 5 households of twenty-one people to eighteen households of seventy-six people. The objective was to show that the strategy could achieve the same density albeit via a very different method of procurement and housing type.

Working with environmental consultants, we deliberated over the appropriate systems for water, sewage, electricity, and heating that could grow over time to supply increasing demand. Inevitably, the pragmatics of cost over environmental performance meant that we rejected many sustainable solutions, such as solar and photovoltaic panels, bio-fuel power units, heat pumps, waste filtration systems, and water supply wells.[150] Given the immense energy demand for heating in the winter, the most practicable approach is to save energy. Shifting household heating from coal to more efficient electrical systems within structures that retain as much heat as possible lessens overall energy consumption, reducing demand on the grid and resulting in less on-site air pollution. Although coal is still the main fuel source at the power stations, they are located away from populated areas. Reducing levels of toxic PM2.5, which is responsible for increasing incidence of respiratory illnesses,[151] would drastically improve air quality and residents' health, reducing school and work sick days.[152]

You need to provide separate septic tanks ... someone's family has an elderly couple and a child while another has six children. They are not going to be happy to pay for someone else's waste.

Batdorj Lusandorj

One of the most contested issues was that of waste sewage. The Ger-Plug-In invoked backlash on social media for its use of a flush system in an area of water scarcity. But composting toilets could not work in Ulaanbaatar, as the essential bacteria cannot survive in winter temperatures, and individual dry latrines require more maintenance and frequent collection, so we opted for a larger collective septic tank between four households and greywater collection systems for toilet flushing. Water delivery is organized by a single inlet pipe which can be connected to a water delivery truck and piped to each household's individual water tank. Thus, each pays rates according to its own consumption yet is spared the inconvenience of trips to the water kiosk. When the density of households increases, the inlet is designed to be converted into a mini kiosk with a shared water tank and small shop.

Infrastructural piping for water and waste is distributed via landscape components that connect existing houses and set out locations for new ones. Each component supports walkways and stairs for residents to access their homes easily and can incorporate paving, gravel, or planting according to their needs.

At many points in the design process the extreme banality of some of the solutions became a frustration. Anything other than the most basic systems was ruled out by the constraints of the site in terms of cost and climate. The resulting infrastructural components are thus stripped down and intensely pragmatic. Nevertheless, they are tangible and within reach.

INCREMENTAL DESIGN MANUAL

The product of our design research on the four-plot clusters is the Incremental Design Manual. Presenting the different housing types and the infrastructural strategy, the aim of the manual is to assist households working collectively to improve their plots. It provides options on how households can improve their living situation based on their needs, family structure, and income. It offers strategies for households in neighboring plots to share the costs of infrastructure and to create a system that allows for growth and future densification. It thus lays out an alternative mechanism of development that complements the ongoing ADB subcenter projects. However, it differs from those projects in its approach, as upgrading is designed to take place insitu while land ownership is retained by residents. It is also incremental and gradual, accommodating families to improve their houses when they are in a financial position to do so. During our surveys with residents, many indicated that they are unhappy with the slow progress of the ADB projects and for the most part cannot see how the projects will benefit them. As an alternative, the manual lays out not a rigid, top-down strategy but one that can adapt and evolve according to such feedback and evaluation. By starting small, with low-risk projects that are achievable and inexpensive, input on their thermal performance and buildability can inform new iterations, resulting in an increased chance of success for the long-term impact and scalability of the project. New technologies, building systems, and different housing types can always be added. In this sense the Manual is a live document, subject to constant editing and adjustments.

TOWARDS A COOPERATIVE MODEL

The argument for incrementality as a strategy for affordable housing in developing regions is not new.[153] Advantages include involving community members in the improvement of their own homes, empowering people to participate in collective decisions, and reducing the reliance on government for funding and implementation. The cost of delivering social housing at a large scale, including its ongoing management, is extremely high for governments, whereas an incremental approach can minimise financial outlay and impact more people. Evidence collected from World Bank evaluation reports demonstrates that minimal investment provided by the state can trigger self-initiated improvements from private owners.[154]

The pioneering work of John Turner in the 1970s highlighted how informal processes could be instrumental in delivering affordable housing.[155] This led to a paradigm shift away from slum clearance programs towards a sites and services approach that aims to enable development through the provision of those aspects that a community could not easily provide themselves. This usually focused on land tenure, infrastructure, and sanitation. By 1983, the World Bank supported over seventy sites and services projects. Multiple methods were tested, usually at a large scale, and inevitably many issues arose. These included land that was allocated too far from jobs, increased corruption that enabled speculators to benefit from subsidised and serviced land, and the difficulty for the poorest families to comply with mandatory house designs. Overall, benefits tended to favour the more financially secure residents rather than the worst off.[156]

In the 1980s, economist Hernando De Soto argued that the legal titling of land and property ownership was a fundamental step in assisting low-income communities to generate wealth, as it allowed them to borrow against this asset. This steered the policy of the World Bank, UN-Habitat, and others in the 1990s towards home ownership, leading to a reliance on mortgage structures and the commodification of housing as an asset.[157] Given the risks of implementation and the long timeframe needed to assess each project, the World Bank shifted away from financing loans for housing construction towards larger-scale economic adjustments for governments.

This shift towards housing as a commodity is of course not only limited to emerging economies but also has shaped a global reliance on bankable finance in the housing market. The liberalization of the housing market via the deregulation of companies providing mortgages, together with the complexity of financial structures linked to the global movement of capital that underlies these products, has become the dominant model for new housing construction. A significant ramification of this model has been periodic global economic distress, notably the sub-prime crisis of 2007 in the US and the 2021 economic defaulting of Chinese property developer Evergrande. Despite this, the promise of an untapped market in developing countries continues to entice international financial institutions focusing on the creation of a housing market in those locations.

Pivoting back to Mongolia, even our incremental urban strategy is premised on residents accessing subsidized low-rate loans for sustainable housing construction. Inevitably, the model is co-opted into the neoliberal framework described above, despite its intentions that lie simply in providing access for sustainable and affordable housing to the most economically challenged residents in Ulaanbaatar. Burdening the lowest-income population with long-term loans is not feasible, given that many households have irregular employment. Moreover, by the time this finance has trickled into actual products offered by local banks it is still expensive, with interest rates higher in developing regions than in the developed world.[158] This is rooted in the priority of limiting risk to financial institutions, a logic which determines that the most impoverished have a less desirable loan capacity than those with more economic means. This contradiction, that the poorest in society have the most expensive means of borrowing, circles back in the form of the continued construction of homes that lack basic sanitation and insulation, and, at scale, will contribute to the ensuing climate crisis for multiple generations.

An alternative model can be found in cooperative organizations. Cooperatives are not new, having emerged at least as early as the Industrial Revolution. They represent a mechanism for members to mutually benefit through collective action. By pooling resources—whether related to finance, land, or labor—individual costs can be lowered, decision making shared, ownership collectivized, and unwanted or speculative development can be controlled. There are many different types of cooperatives within the housing sector that relate to the acquisition and management of land and homes, the construction process, and financing. The scope of this

The liberalization of the housing market via the deregulation of companies providing mortgages, together with the complexity of financial structures linked to the global movement of capital that underlies these products, has become the dominant model for new housing construction.

publication does not extend to a detailed assessment of each model or to the initiation of a cooperative structure for Ulaanbaatar. However, two existing models show potential for the ger districts.[159]

Community land trusts allow land to be collectively owned by members while houses themselves remain under individual ownership, each with a tenancy agreement for the common land held by the trust. This means that the trust, operating as a democratically governed nonprofit, can allocate space for housing and organize the development process. Collectively, the trust can decide to construct surplus housing as rental units, or to invest in infrastructure, community services, or public space improvements. It could be a mechanism to initiate our four-plot proposal by bringing the land of four households under collective ownership and using this as collateral to kickstart the infrastructural improvements of sewage and water, which in turn could lead to individual investment into housing types that suit each families' needs.

Another option could be a mutual aid housing cooperative. This model emerged in the 1960s in Latin America and involves the collective ownership of both land and housing. Under this model each community member participates in housing construction and the administration of the cooperative, thereby reducing costs significantly. It requires specialist training and education and is often supported by other entities to supply technical assistance.[160] This model embeds long-term capacity-building across generations as every member must contribute.

Mongolia, in fact, has a long history of cooperative organization, albeit state controlled during the Soviet period. This legacy may serve to make the idea and adoption of cooperative models more amenable to residents. Currently it is too premature to say. However, any cooperative model would require assistance from government or the nonprofit sector to initiate and organize itself, as well as to train members with financial, legal, and construction skills and expertise. The Incremental Design Manual can support this process, providing a set of ingredients that enable residents to improve their plots both individually and collectively. Unlike other approaches to informal development, the Manual offers a strategy for insitu upgrading that accommodates incremental growth and collective improvements to shared plots. It operates at a small scale to promote the mutual benefits of four plots working together as the base unit for all further transformation. In other words, the design logic engenders its own collectively organized administration. Implementing the Manual, working with just four families at a time, could provide the first steps to enable a future cooperative to form.

ӨРГӨТГӨН САЙЖРУУЛАХ БҮТЭЭН БАЙГУУЛАЛТ ГАРЫН АВЛАГА
INCREMENTAL DEVELOPMENT MANUAL

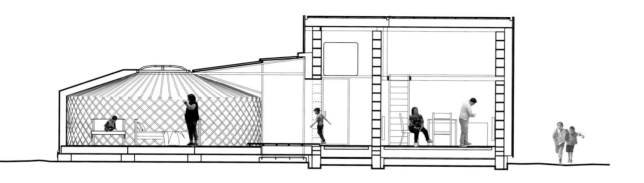

Энэхүү гарын авлага нь таны өрхийн хэрэгцээ ба боломжит төсөвт тохирсон орон сууцны барилгыг барьж нийлүүлэх үйлчилгээг санал болгож байгааг танилцуулга юм. Энд янз бүрийн өрөөний зохион байгуулалттай олон үе шаттайгаар баригдах загваруудыг танилцуулна.

Загвар бүрийг гэртэй холбож өргөтгөж болох ба энэ нь эрчим хүчний хэмнэлт, шүршүүр, бие засах газар, гал тогоо, халаагуур гэх зэрэг давуу талуудыг агуулсан байна. Хэрэв та аль хэдийн байшинтай эсвэл баригдаж байгаа бол дэд бүтцийн асуудлыг шийдэхэд бид танд туслах юм. Та хөршүүдтэйгээ нийлж загвар, гадна талбайн тохижилтыг шийдсэн дэд бүтцийн холболтыг хийлгэх ажил үйлчилгээг биднээс авч болно. Үүнчлэн таны сонгосон загвар/ бүтээгдхүүний бүдүүвч төсвийг бодож банкнаас бага хүүтэй ногоон зээл авахад туслах юм.

This manual consists of different housing components that are designed to respond to your household needs and your available budget. It includes models that can be built in stages and have different spatial arrangements.

Each model can integrate a standard ger as an additional room that can be added or removed. Each house is energy efficient, and contains a shower, toilet, kitchen, and heating. If you already have a house or are in the process of construction, we have products that can help you add the infrastructure that you need. This manual shows you how you can work with your neighbors to upgrade your plots together, including better servicing, access, and landscaping. It provides estimated costs and shows you how you can access low-interest green loans from the banks.

КАТАЛОГ
CATALOGUE

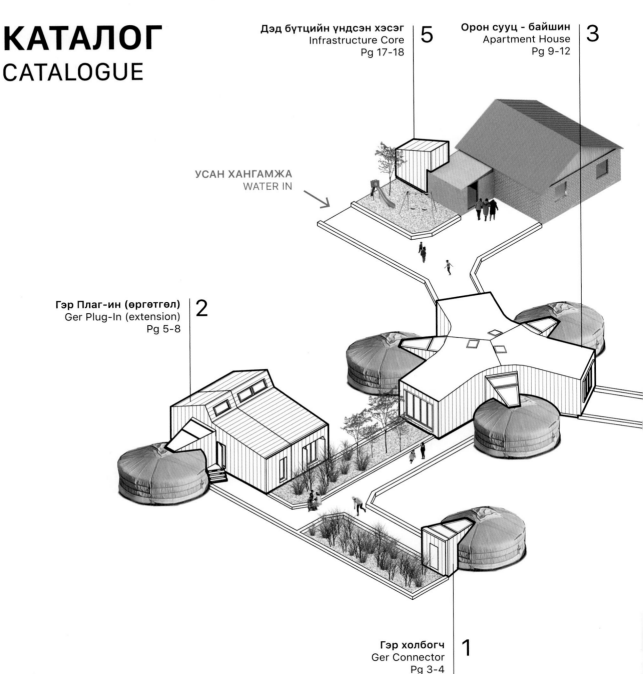

Дэд бүтцийн үндсэн хэсэг
Infrastructure Core
Pg 17-18
5

Орон сууц - байшин
Apartment House
Pg 9-12
3

Гэр Плаг-ин (өргөтгөл)
Ger Plug-In (extension)
Pg 5-8
2

Гэр холбогч
Ger Connector
Pg 3-4
1

УСАН ХАНГАМЖА
WATER IN

Бидний бүтээгдхүүний жагсаалтад энгийн гэр холбогчоос эхлээд орон сууцны том овор бүхий байшин хүртэл багтдаг. Эхний алхам бол таны хэрэгцээ, төсөвт тулгуурлан байшин эсвэл дэд бүтцийн шинэчлэлтийг сонгох асуудал юм. Мөн та бүтээгдхүүнийг өөрийн хөрөнгөөр худалдан авах боломжтой эсэх, эсвэл нэмэлт санхүүжилт шаардлагатай эсэхийг тодруулна. Хэрэв та зээл авах шаардлагатай бол бидний бүтээгдхүүн бага хүүтэй зээлд хамрагдах боломжтой тул таныг ногоон орон сууцны зээлтэй холбоход тусална. Бид танай талбай дээр очиж шинэ байшин барих хамгийн тохиромжтой байршлыг төлөвлөх болно. Та бидэнтэй худалдан авах гэрээ байгуулж, банктай зээлийн гэрээгээ тохиролцсоны дараа бид таны байшинг барьж гүйцэтгэнэ.

The different components range from a simple ger connector to a large apartment house. The first step is to select a house or infrastructure upgrade based on your needs and your budget. Consider if you can fully purchase the product or will require additional financing. If you need to borrow, we can assist in linking you to green mortgages as our products are eligible for these low-interest loans. We will visit your plot to plan the best location for your new house. Once you have signed the purchase agreement with us and arranged the loan agreement with the bank, we will build your house.

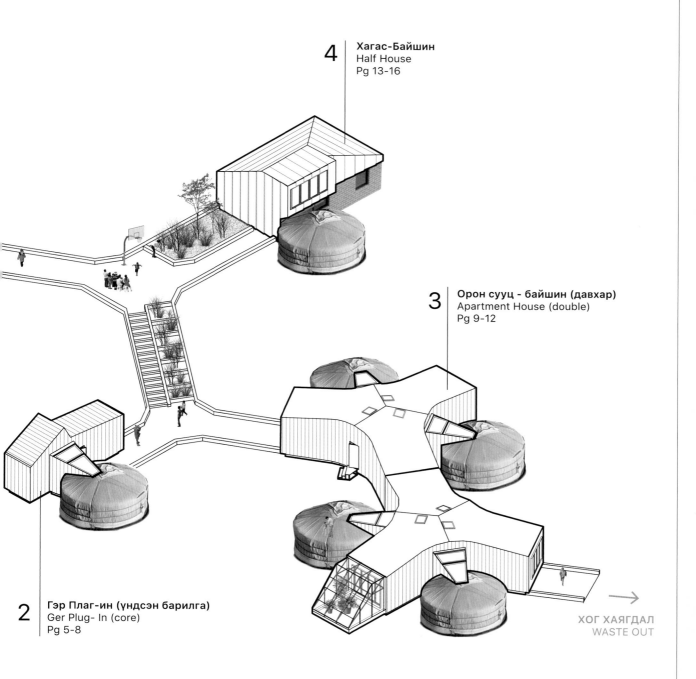

4 | Хагас-Байшин
Half House
Pg 13-16

3 | Орон сууц - байшин (давхар)
Apartment House (double)
Pg 9-12

2 | Гэр Плаг-ин (үндсэн барилга)
Ger Plug- In (core)
Pg 5-8

ХОГ ХАЯГДАЛ
WASTE OUT

ГЭР ХОЛБОГЧ
GER CONNECTOR

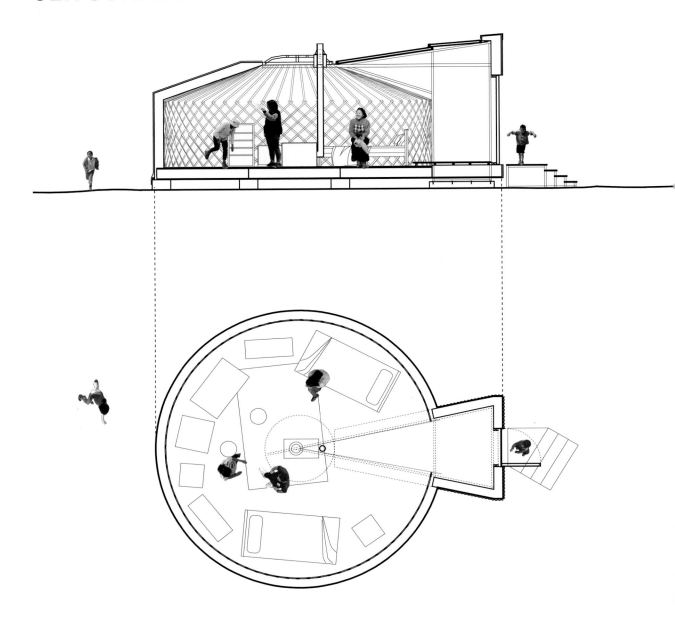

Гэр холбогч нь дулаан алдагдахаас сэргийлж таны гэрт орох хаалга болон нэмэлт дулаалга хийж өгнө. Энэхүү бүтэц нь төв баганыг арилгаж ашигтай талбайг ихэсгэдэг. Энэ нь манай үйлчилгээний хамгийн жижиг нэгж бөгөөд шугам шулжээнд холбох, орон зай талбайг томсгох дараагийн шат болох гэрийн өргөтгөл рүү хялбархан холбогдох боломжийг бүрдүүлнэ.

The Ger Connector provides a threshold and additional insulation to your ger to prevent heat loss. The structure enables you to remove the central column making an open living space. It is the most basic unit and can easily extend into the Ger Plug-In to provide infrastructure and additional space. The Ger Connector can also be added to an existing house or the Apartment House for extra living space.

1 Одоо байгаа гэр
Traditional Ger

2 Гэр холбогч
Ger Connector

3 Холболтын сонголтууд
Connection Options

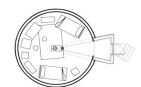

Одоо байгаа
байшин
Existing House

Гэр Плаг-ин
Ger Plug-In

Орон сууцны
байшин
Apartment House

Жижиг гэр бүл
Small single family

Жижиг гэр бүл
Small single family

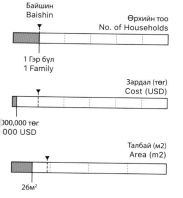

Байшин
Baishin

Өрхийн тоо
No. of Households

1 Гэр бүл
1 Family

Зардал (төг)
Cost (USD)

000,000 төг
000 USD

Талбай (м2)
Area (m2)

26м²

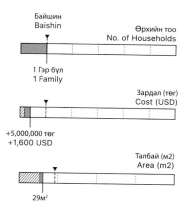

Байшин
Baishin

Өрхийн тоо
No. of Households

1 Гэр бүл
1 Family

Зардал (төг)
Cost (USD)

+5,000,000 төг
+1,600 USD

Талбай (м2)
Area (m2)

29м²

ГЭР ПЛАГ-ИН
GER PLUG-IN

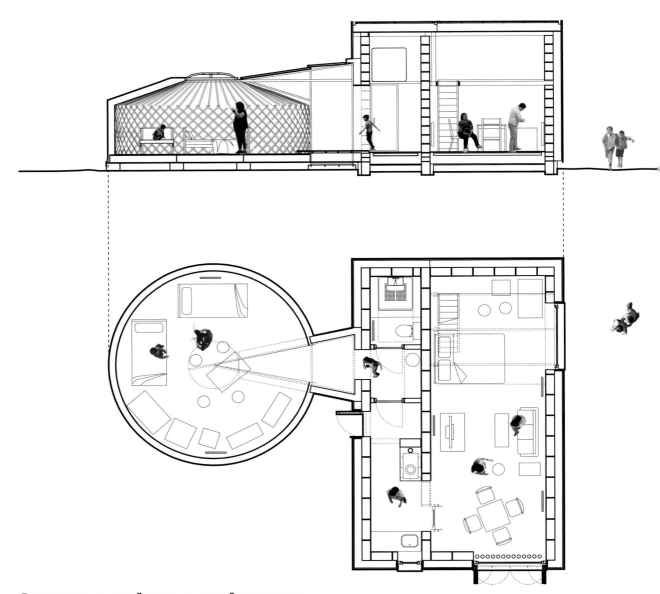

Гэр өргөтгөл нь гэрийг хоер үе шаттайгаар томсгох боломжийг олгодог. Эхний шат болох Ger Plug-In Core буюу үндсэн хэсэг нь шүршүүр, бие засах газар, гал тогоо, цахилгаан халаагуур зэрэг зайлшгүй шаардлагатай хэрэгслээр хангадаг. Хоер дахь шат болох залгаас өргөтгөл нь хажуу тийш сунгаж зочны өрөө, хоолны өрөө, унтлагын өрөөг нэмнэ. Таны гэрийг унтлагын өрөө, ажлын өрөө, тоглоомын өрөө болгон ашиглаж болно. Хэрэв танд нөөц бололцоо байгаа бөгөөд үе шаттайгаар барих шаардлагагүй бол нэгдсэн дэд бүтэцтэй Гэр Хаусыг гэртэй болон гэргүйгээр барьж болох юм. Байшингийн фасадыг өөрийн сонголтоор янз бүрийн өнгөт мод болох байгалийн, шатаасан хүрэн, хар үнсэн мод зэргээр гадарлаж болно.

The Ger Plug-In allows you to expand your ger in two stages. The first stage, Ger Plug-In Core, provides the essentials: a shower, toilet, kitchen, and electrical heating. The second stage, Ger Plug-In Extension, extends sideways to provide a living room, dining area and raised sleeping deck. Your ger can be used as a spare bedroom, study, or playroom. If you have available resources and don't need to build in phases, the Ger House with integrated infrastructure can be used with or without a ger. The house can be clad in different coloured timber based on your preference: choose from natural wood, burnt umber, or ash black

1
Одоо байгаа гэр
Ger and Connector

2
Гэр Плаг-ин (үндсэн барилга)
Ger Plug-In (Core)

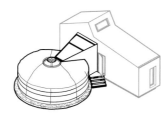

3
Гэр Плаг-ин (өргөтгөл)
Ger Plug-In (Extension)

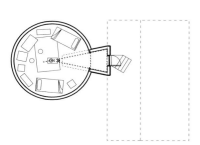

+11.8m²

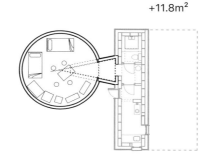

+28m²

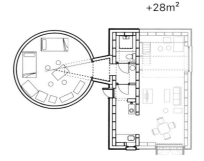

Жижиг гэр бүл
Small single family

Жижиг гэр бүл
Small single family

Олон хүүхэдтэй өрх толгойлсон гэр бүл
Single family with multiple children

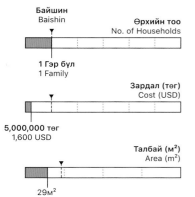

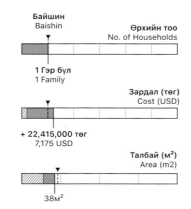

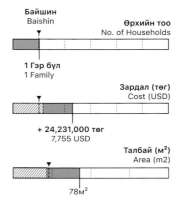

| Байшин Baishin | | Өрхийн тоо No. of Households |

1 Гэр бүл
1 Family

| | Зардал (төг) Cost (USD) |

5,000,000 төг
1,600 USD

| | Талбай (м²) Area (m²) |

29м²

| Байшин Baishin | | Өрхийн тоо No. of Households |

1 Гэр бүл
1 Family

| | Зардал (төг) Cost (USD) |

+ 22,415,000 төг
7,175 USD

| | Талбай (м²) Area (m2) |

38м²

| Байшин Baishin | | Өрхийн тоо No. of Households |

1 Гэр бүл
1 Family

| | Зардал (төг) Cost (USD) |

+ 24,231,000 төг
7,755 USD

| | Талбай (м²) Area (m2) |

78м²

ГЭР ПЛАГ-ИН
GER PLUG-IN

1

1-р шат: Гэр холбогч: гэрийн үүд ба сайн чанарын дулаалга.

Phase 1: Ger Connector: a new entry threshold and better insulation.

2

2-р шат: Гэр өргөтгөлийн үндсэн хэсэг: гал тогоо, усны халаагч, зуух, шүршүүр, жорлон бүхий ахуйн хэрэглээний хэсэг.

Phase 2: Ger Plug-In Core: infrastructural bar with kitchen, hot water boiler, stove, shower, and toilet.

3 **3-р шат: Гэр өргөтгөлийн сунгалт хэсэг:** нэмэлтээр зочны болон хоолны өрөө, унтлаганы өрөө бүхий дээврийн хөндий барих.

Phase 3: Ger Plug-In Extension: additional living and dining room and raised loft for sleeping.

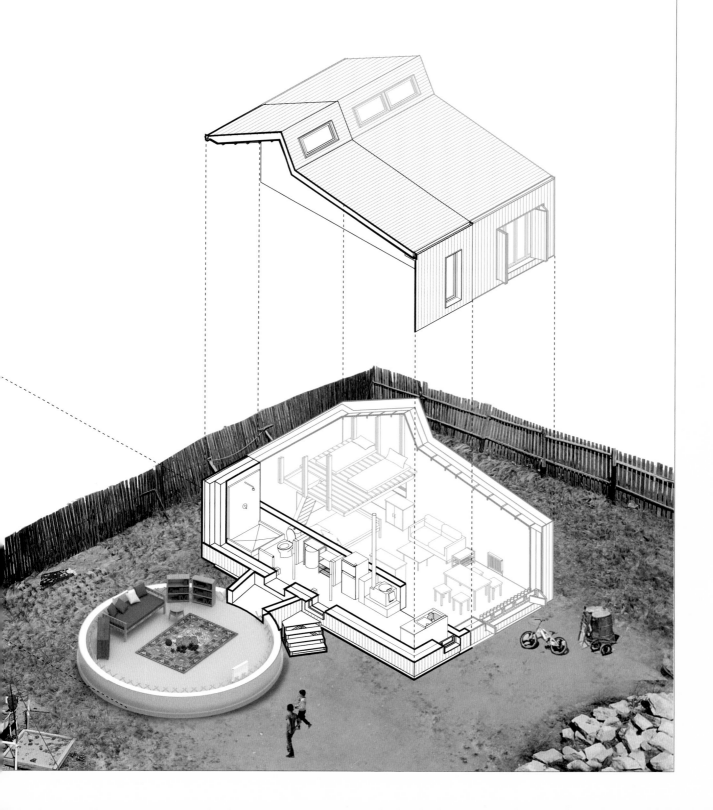

ОРОН СУУЦНЫ БАЙШИН
APARTMENT HOUSE

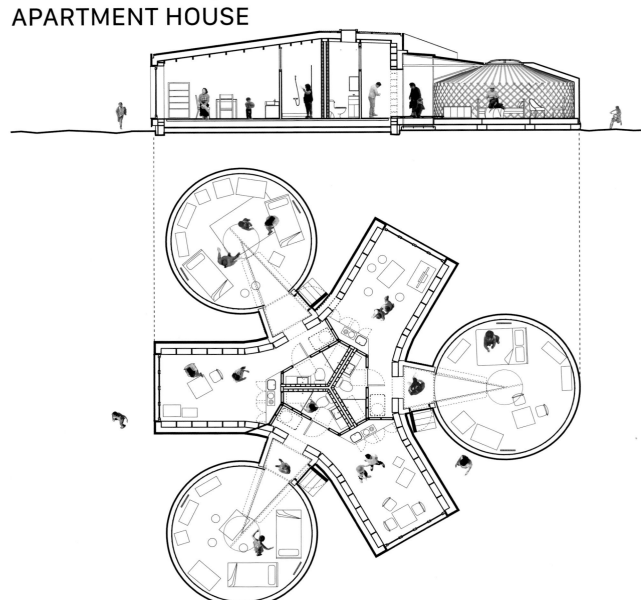

Орон сууц - байшин нь газраа чөлөөлөхгүйгээр орон сууцанд амьдрах бүх давуу талыг олгодог. Үүнийг нэг том байшин, хоёр жижиг хэсэгтэй нэг том байр, гурван жижиг орон сууц гэх мэтээр төлөвлөж болно. Нэгж бүрийг гэртэй холбох боломжтой бөгөөд нэмэгдэл барилгыг хангах дэд бүтцийн нөөцтэй байхаар төлөвлөгдсөн байна. Хэрэв та хүсвэл өргөтгөлийг бусдад түрээслэж нэмэлт орлого олох боломжтой. Эсвэл та үр удамтайгаа нэг том байшинд амьдарч болох юм. Мөн гэр хэсгийг дангаар нь унтлагын өрөө болгож бусад талбайг амьдрах, хооллох, чөлөөт цагаа өнгөрүүлэх орон зай болгож ашиглах гэх зэрэг боломжтой.

All the advantages of apartment living without giving up your land. The apartment house contains three separate units each with a shower, toilet, heating system and kitchen. Each unit can attach to a ger providing additional space and capacity for growth. If you are the landowner, you can rent out the additional units to other families bringing you additional income. Alternatively, you could share the house with different generations of your family. Or you could use each ger as a bedroom and enjoy a large living and dining space.

1 нэг өрх
One Household

2 2 өрх
Two Households

3 3 өрх
Three Households

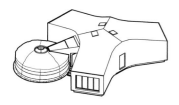

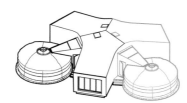

54m²
(+26m²)

36м²
(+26m²)

18m²
(+26m²)

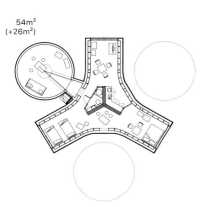

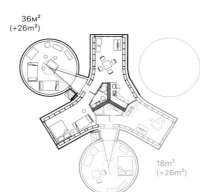

18m²
(+26m²)

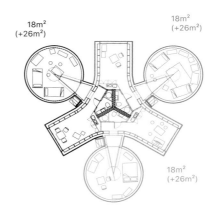

18m²
(+26m²)

18m²
(+26m²)

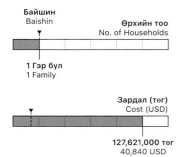

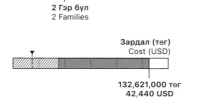

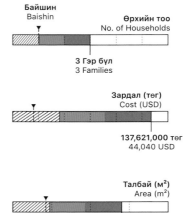

Жижиг гэр бүл
One large household

Жижиг гэр бүл
Two households

Олон хүүхэдтэй өрх толгойлсон гэр бүл
Up to three households

Байшин
Baishin

Өрхийн тоо
No. of Households

Байшин
Baishin

Өрхийн тоо
No. of Households

Байшин
Baishin

Өрхийн тоо
No. of Households

1 Гэр бүл
1 Family

2 Гэр бүл
2 Families

3 Гэр бүл
3 Families

Зардал (төг)
Cost (USD)

Зардал (төг)
Cost (USD)

Зардал (төг)
Cost (USD)

127,621,000 төг
40,840 USD

132,621,000 төг
42,440 USD

137,621,000 төг
44,040 USD

Талбай (м²)
Area (m²)

Талбай (м²)
Area (m²)

Талбай (м²)
Area (m²)

80м²

106м²

132м²

ОРОН СУУЦНЫ БАЙШИН
APARTMENT HOUSE

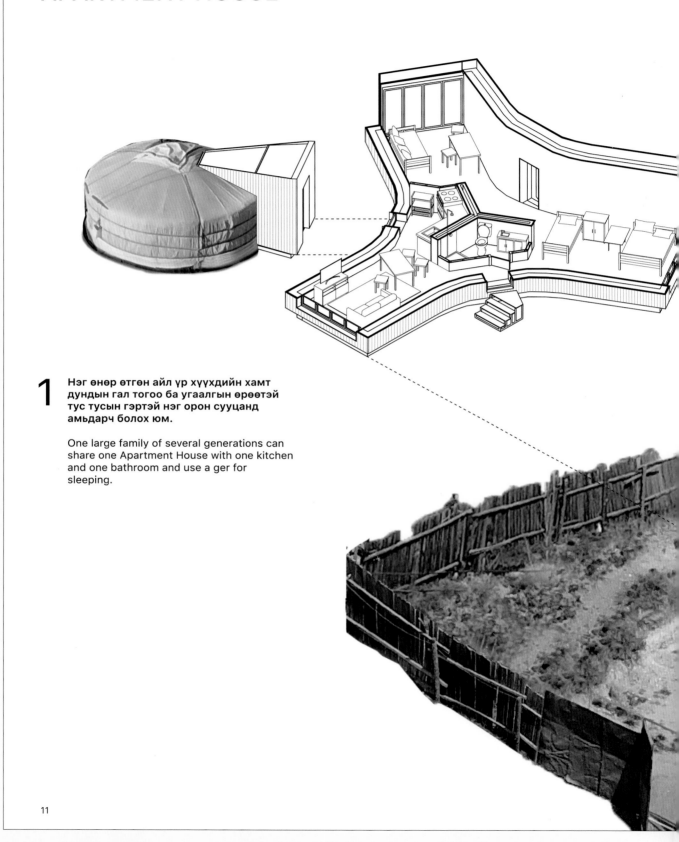

1 Нэг өнөр өтгөн айл үр хүүхдийн хамт дундын гал тогоо ба угаалгын өрөөтэй тус тусын гэртэй нэг орон сууцанд амьдарч болох юм.

One large family of several generations can share one Apartment House with one kitchen and one bathroom and use a ger for sleeping.

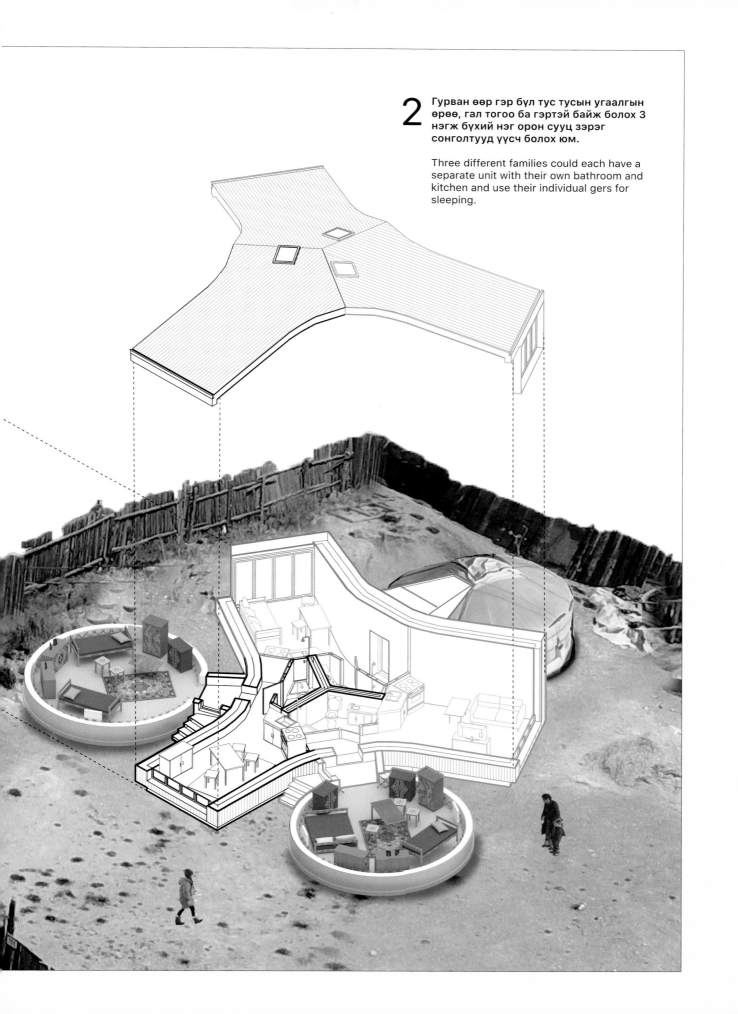

2 Гурван өөр гэр бүл тус тусын угаалгын өрөө, гал тогоо ба гэртэй байж болох 3 нэгж бүхий нэг орон сууц зэрэг сонголтууд үүсч болох юм.

Three different families could each have a separate unit with their own bathroom and kitchen and use their individual gers for sleeping.

ХАГАС-БАЙШИН
HALF HOUSE

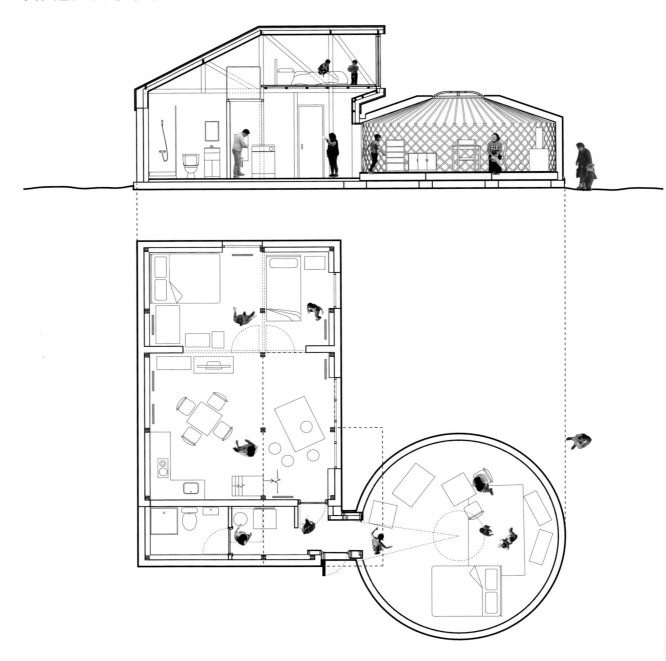

Хагас - Байшин нь байшингаа бүрэн барьж дуусгах боломжийг олгодог. Энэ нь ариун цэврийн болон сайжруулсан дулаалалттай хэсэг ба фермийн бүтээц бүхий дээврээс бүрддэг. Байшин гэрийг шувуун дээврээр холбож энд үүсэх орон зайг хүүхдийн унтлагын өрөө эсвэл тоглоомын талбай болгон ашиглаж болох юм

The Half House allows you to complete the construction of your house. It consists of an additional trussroof and infrastructure module that can provide sanitation and improved thermal performance. The pitched roof provides a loft space for sleeping, and the house can connect to your existing ger that can be used as a kids' bedroom or playspace.

1

Одоо байгаа хагас баригдсан байшин
Existing House

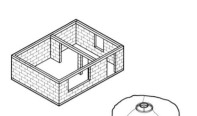

2

Одоо байгаа хагас
Half House

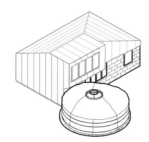

+10м² Дэд бүтэц
+20м² Дээврийн талбай

+10m² infrastructure
+20m² loft space

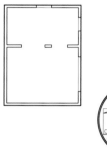

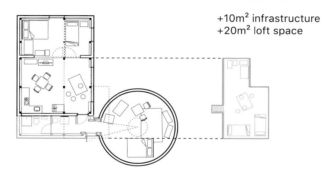

Жижиг гэр бүл
Single family

Single multi-generation family

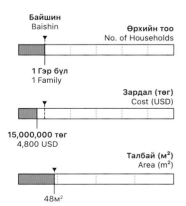

Байшин
Baishin

Өрхийн тоо
No. of Households

1 Гэр бүл
1 Family

Зардал (төг)
Cost (USD)

15,000,000 төг
4,800 USD

Талбай (м²)
Area (m²)

48м²

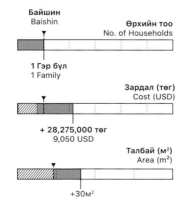

Байшин
Baishin

Өрхийн тоо
No. of Households

1 Гэр бүл
1 Family

Зардал (төг)
Cost (USD)

+ 28,275,000 төг
9,050 USD

Талбай (м²)
Area (m²)

+30м²

ХАГАС-БАЙШИН
HALF HOUSE

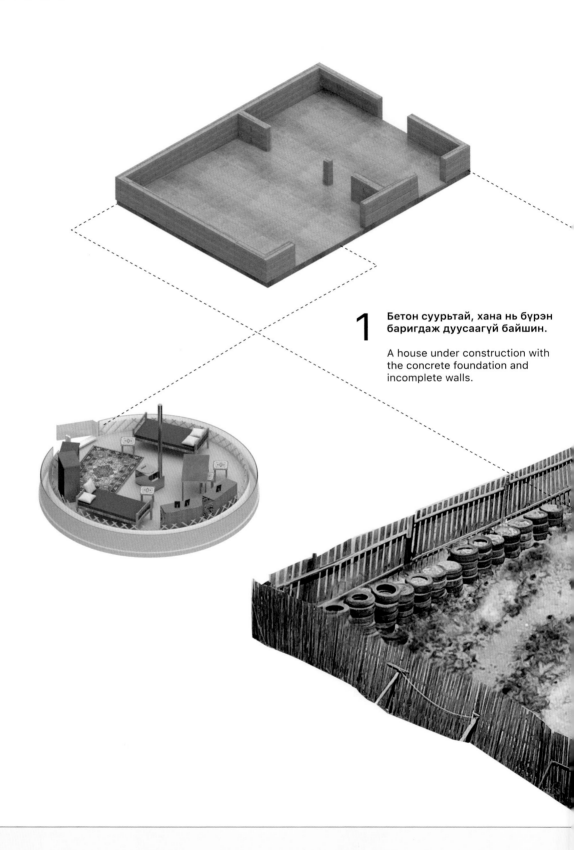

1   **Бетон суурьтай, хана нь бүрэн баригдаж дуусаагүй байшин.**

A house under construction with the concrete foundation and incomplete walls.

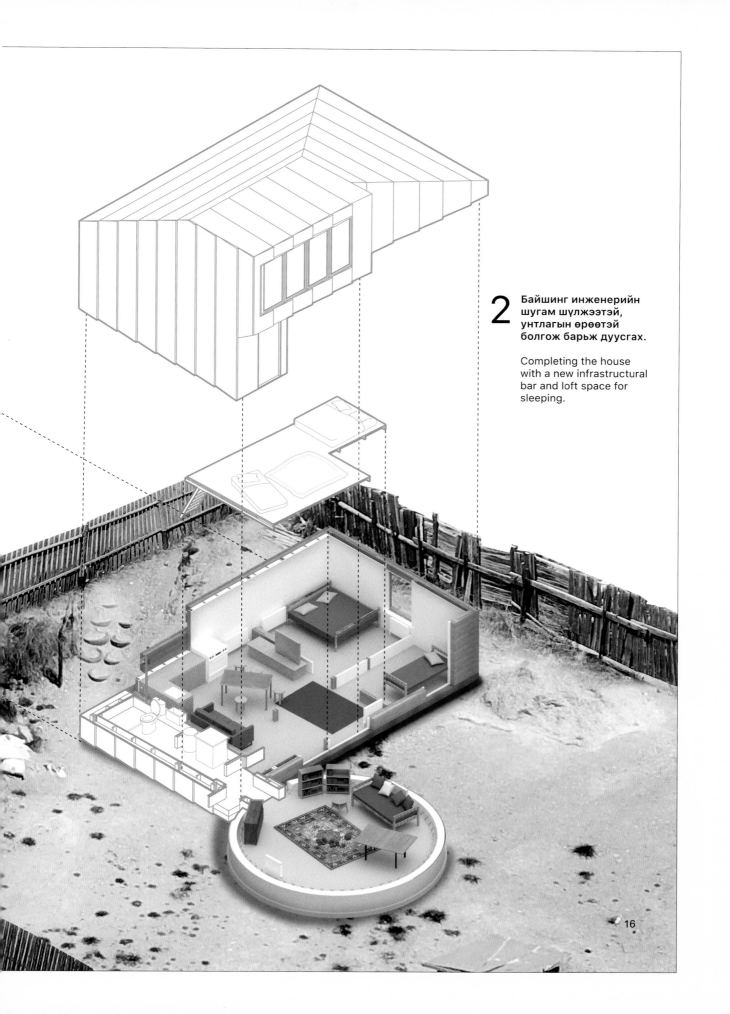

2 Байшинг инженерийн шугам шүлжээтэй, унтлагын өрөөтэй болгож барьж дуусгах.

Completing the house with a new infrastructural bar and loft space for sleeping.

ДЭД БҮТЦИЙН ҮНДСЭН ХЭСЭГ
INFRASTRUCTURAL CORE

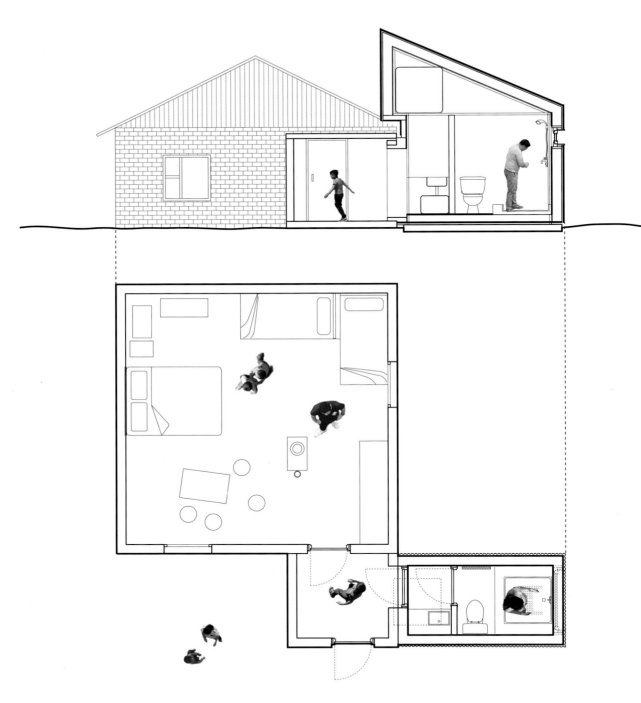

Дэд бүтцийн үндсэн хэсэг нь танд одоо байгаа байшиндаа бие засах газар, шүршүүр, усны сав нэмэх боломжийг олгоно. Энэ нь дулааны алдагдлаас сэргийлэх үүднээс шинэ дулаалга бүхий хаалга барина.

The Infrastructural Core module allows you to add a toilet, shower, and water tank to your existing house. It also creates a new entrance threshold to prevent heat loss.

1   Одоо байгаа гэр
Existing House

2   Дэд бүтцийн үндсэн хэсэг
Infrastructural Core

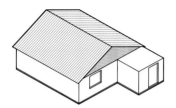

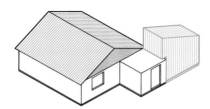

Жижиг гэр бүл
Single family

Жижиг гэр бүл
Single family

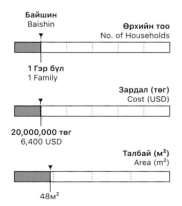

Байшин
Baishin

Өрхийн тоо
No. of Households

1 Гэр бүл
1 Family

Зардал (төг)
Cost (USD)

20,000,000 төг
6,400 USD

Талбай (м²)
Area (m²)

48м²

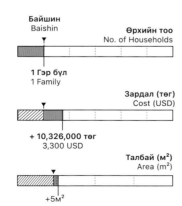

Байшин
Baishin

Өрхийн тоо
No. of Households

1 Гэр бүл
1 Family

Зардал (төг)
Cost (USD)

+ 10,326,000 төг
3,300 USD

Талбай (м²)
Area (m²)

+5м²

ГАДНА ТАЛБАЙН ДЭД БҮТЭЦ
LANDSCAPE INFRASTRUCTURE

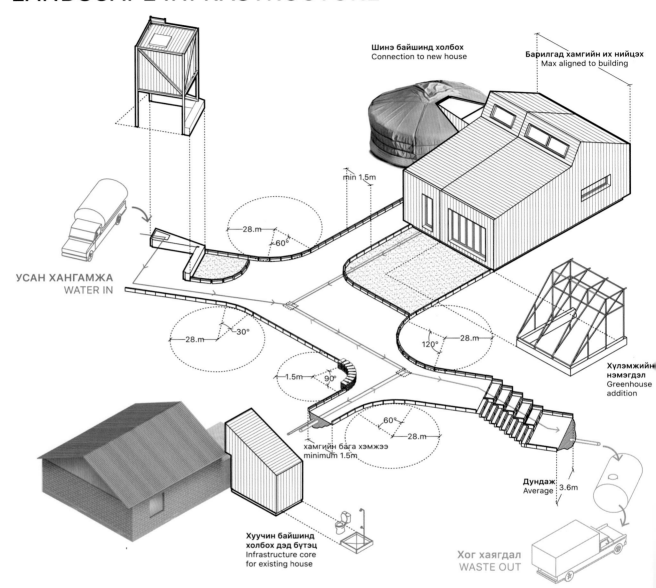

Шинэ байшинд холбох
Connection to new house

Барилгад хамгийн их нийцэх
Max aligned to building

min 1.5m

28.m
60°

УСАН ХАНГАМЖА
WATER IN

28.m
30°

1.5m
90°

28.m
120°

Хүлэмжийн нэмэгдэл
Greenhouse addition

60°
28.m

хамгийн бага хэмжээ
minimum 1.5m

Дундаж
Average 3.6m

Хог хаягдал
WASTE OUT

Хуучин байшинд холбох дэд бүтэц
Infrastructure core for existing house

Энэ нь бохирын системийг барилгын талбайд байршуулах инженерийн шугам шүлжээ юм. Нэгдүгээрт, талбайн өндөр цэгт ус түгээгүүрийн машинтай холбох ус дамжуулах хоолойн эхлэх цэгийг байршуулж, талбайн доод цэгт бохир ус цуглуулах септик танкийг суулгана. Ус дамжуулах хоолойг хөлдөөхгүйн тулд зузаан дулаалгатайгаар газар доор угсрах ба барилгын бохирын системд холбогдох шугамыг гадна талбайн тохижилтын элементүүд болох налуу газарт зориулсан шат, олон нийтийн мод ургамал тарих талбай, хүнсний ногооны талбай, тоглоомын талбай зэргээс сонгож далдлах юм Хөршүүдтэйгээ хамтран ажилласнаар дэд бүтцийн шугам шүлжээ, нийтийн эзэмшлийн талбайн хамгийн зөв шийдлийг бага зардалд багтаан шийдэх боломжтой.

These components help guide how you can provide infrastructural connection to your plots for water and sewage waste collection. Firstly, the water inlet pipe should be established at the high point of the site for truck water delivery, and septic tanks located at the low point to collect waste-water. The pipes are carried underground in thick insulation to avoid freezing. Select from the different landscape pieces to connect existing houses and new houses to the new infrastructure. These include staircases for sloped ground, public spaces for planting, vegetable gardens, and play areas. By working with your neighbors you can decide on the best solution for your plots and share the costs of the infrastructure and common spaces.

1

УСНЫ ОРОЛТ
Water inlet

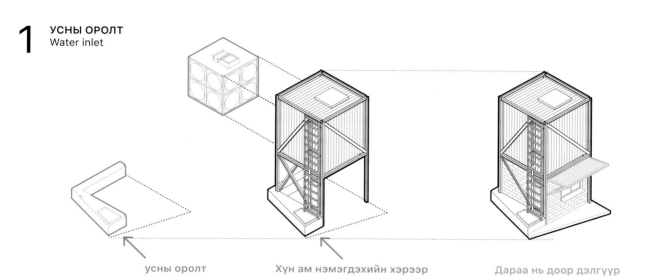

усны оролт
Water Inlet

Хүн ам нэмэгдэхийн хэрээр усны танкийг томсгох
Expands to larger water tank when population increases

Дараа нь доор дэлгүүр нэмж оруулах боломжтой
Infill to create shop underneath

2

Газрын хэсгүүдтэй холбох
Connect with ground pieces

3

Тулгуур налуу газар
Retain slope

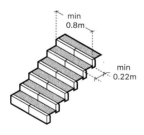

min 0.8m

min 0.22m

Шат
Stair

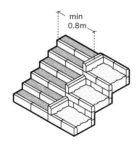

min 0.8m

Шат ба мод ургамал тарих талбай
Stair and planting

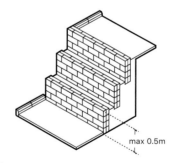

max 0.5m

Тулгуур хана
Retaining wall

4

Газрын дүүргэлтийг сонгоно
Choose ground fill

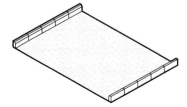

Хайрган дүүргэлт
Gravel fill

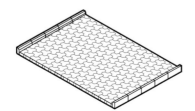

Явган замын хавтангаар бүрэн дүүргэх
Full paving

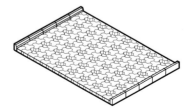

Явган замын хавтангаар хагас дүүргэх
Half paving

ХУВИЛБАР 1
SCENARIO 1

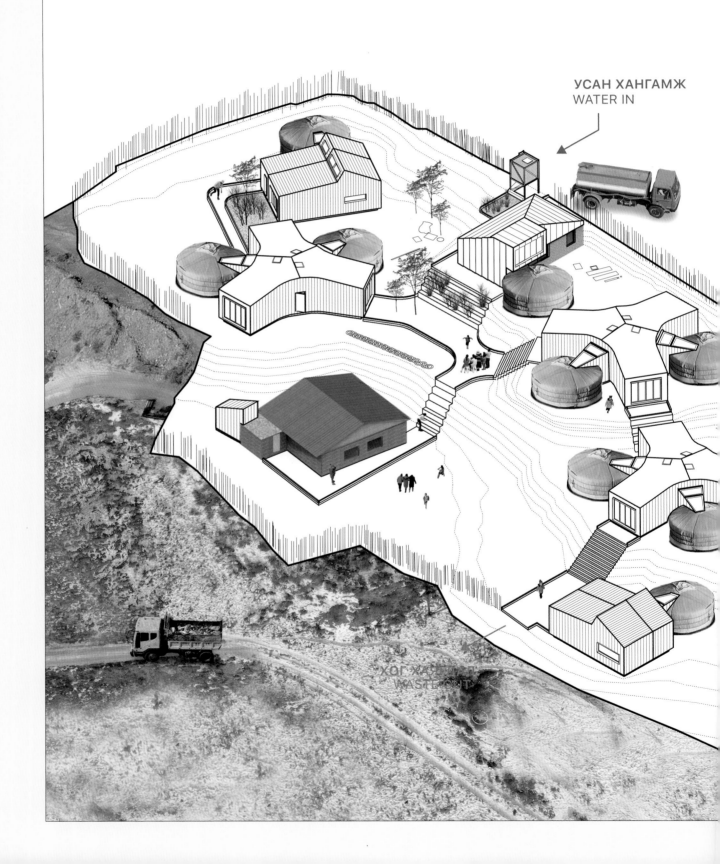

УСАН ХАНГАМЖ
WATER IN

ХОГ ХАЯГДАЛ
WASTE OUT

Дараах гурван жишээгээр 4 барилгын кластерыг өөр өөрөөр хэрхэн төлөвлэж болохыг үзүүлнэ. Хөршүүд хамтарч дэд бүтцийг төлөвлөх, олон нийтийн болон гадна талбайг тохижуулах цаашид өргөтгөж томсгох боломжтой гэр бүлийн болон түрээсийн орон сууц-байшинг хэрхэн барьж болохыг жишээгээр харуулна,

Хуучин эсвэл дутуу баригдсан барилгыг холбож өндрөөс авах усны оролт, нам доор байрлах бохирын танкийг багтаасан инженерийн шугам шүлжээ ба гадна талбайн тохижилт бүхий ажил үйлчилгээ байж болно. -Энэ сүлжээг шинээр барилга нэмэх мөн ирээдүйд бий болох хэрэгцээний хирээр өргөтгөх боломж бүхий шугам шүлжээний нөөцтэйгээр төлөвлөнө.

The following three examples show different ways to organize a cluster of four plots. It shows how you can work with your neighbors to set up infrastructure, access walkways, planting areas, and plan for the future growth of additional houses that you can rent to new tenants or use for your family.

The landscape and infrastructure components connect the existing house and half-completed house to the upper road for a water inlet and the lower road for septic collection. New houses plug into this network and the infrastructure expands to allow for future growth.

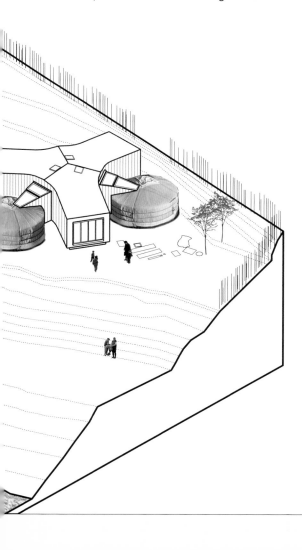

1 одоо байгаа хашаа
Existing khashaas

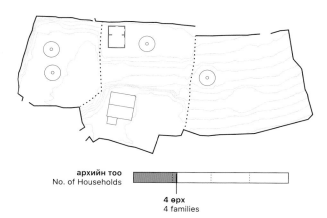

архийн тоо
No. of Households

4 өрх
4 families

2 Шинэ дэд бүтцийн ажлыг нуруу бий болгох
шинэ байшин барих
Build infrastructure
Build new houses

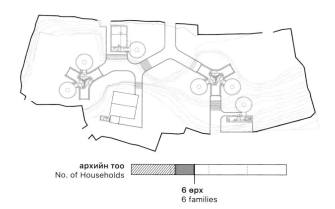

архийн тоо
No. of Households

6 өрх
6 families

3 шинэ байшин барих
Байшинг өргөтгөх
Build new houses
Extend existing houses

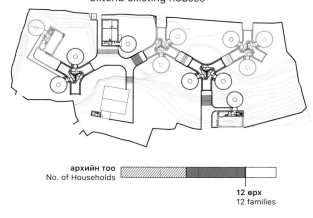

архийн тоо
No. of Households

12 өрх
12 families

ХУВИЛБАР 2
SCENARIO 2

Өндрөөс нам руу чиглэсэн 4 орон сууцны хоорондох төв хашааны заагийг одоо байгаа байшингууд болон зэрэгцээ замуудыг холбосон байдлаар дэд бүтцийн талбайгаар солих ажил үйлчилгээ байж болох юм. Газрын түвшний дээд тал нь усны оролттой хэсэг, доод талд нь бохир усны септик танк байрлана. Энэ талбай нь шугам шүлжээнээс гадна шат, мод тарих талбай, нийтийн эзэмшлийн талбайтай байх юм. Эхэлж холбогдож байгаа гэр бүлүүд өөрсдийн хэрэгцээнд хамгийн сайн тохирох байшингийн төрлийг сонгох боломжтой. Дэд бүтцийн нөөцтэй байгаа газар нь шинээр шилжин ирэгсдийн сонирхлыг татахуйц шинэ орон сууц барьж, түрээслүүлж, газар эзэмшигчдэд нэмэлт орлого авчрах боломжтой гэсэн үг юм. Гудамжны дагуу өргөтгөл хийснээр дэлгүүрүүд ба ажлын байр бий болно.

The infrastructural spine replaces the fence boundary between four plots connecting the existing houses and parallel roads. A water inlet is provided at the top and waste-water and sewage are collected at the bottom. The spine provides stairs, planting areas and shared public spaces. The access to infrastructure means that the land is attractive to new migrants and so new housing can be built and rented to bring additional revenue to landowners.

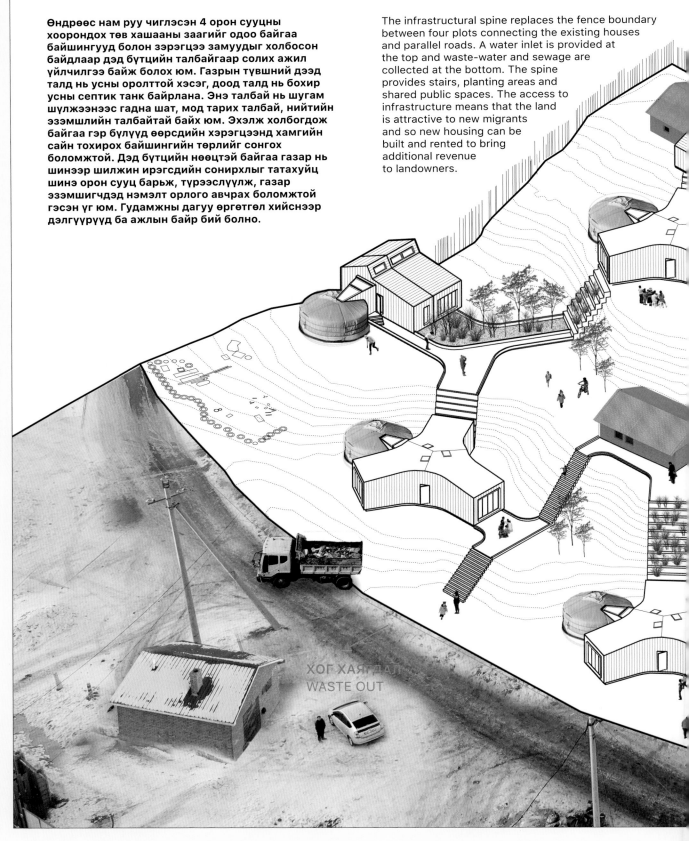

ХОГ ХАЯГДАЛ ХОГ
WASTE OUT

УСАН ХАНГАМЖ
WATER IN

1 одоо байгаа хашаа
Existing khashaas

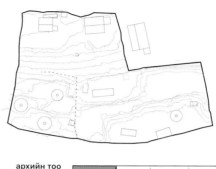

архийн тоо
No. of Households

6 өрх
6 families

2 Шинэ дэд бүтцийн ажлыг нуруу
бий болгох
шинэ байшин барих
Build infrastructure
Build new houses

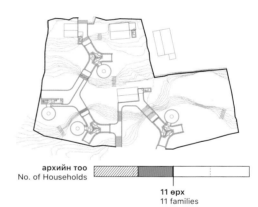

архийн тоо
No. of Households

11 өрх
11 families

3 шинэ байшин барих
Байшинг өргөтгөх
Build new houses
Extend existing houses

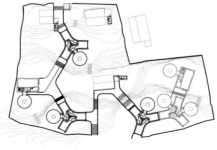

архийн тоо
No. of Households

14 өрх
14 families

ХУВИЛБАР 3
SCENARIO 3

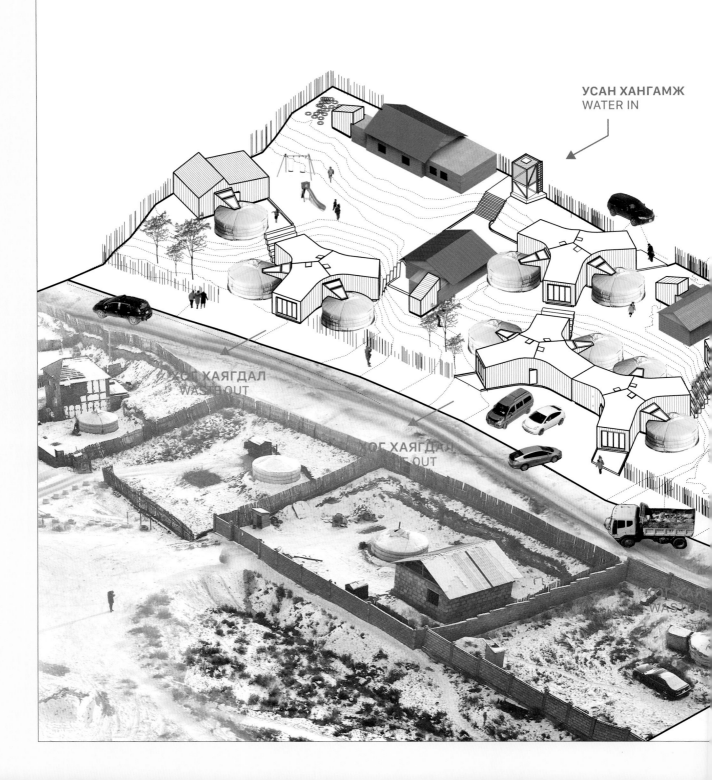

УСАН ХАНГАМЖ
WATER IN

ХОГ ХАЯГДАЛ
WASTE OUT

ХОГ ХАЯГДАЛ
WASTE OUT

Энэхүү стратеги нь дээд ба доод гудамжны хоорондох шугам шүлжээг өндөр налуу хэсэгт усны оролтын шугам, доод хэсэгт нь септик танкийг байршуулах замаар шийдэх юм. Энэ нь орон сууцны блокийн хооронд цэцэг ургамал, тоглоомын талбай бүхий хамтын эзэмшлийн талбайг үүсгэнэ.

The overall strategy is to weave the infrastructure between the top and bottom roads with water inlets at the higher gradient and septic collection at the lower. This creates pockets of shared open space between plots that can be used as a collective resource for planting or play areas.

1 одоо байгаа хашаа
Existing khashaas

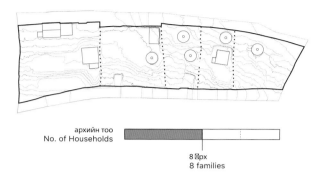

архийн тоо
No. of Households

8 👤px
8 families

2 Шинэ дэд бүтцийн ажлыг нуруу бий болгох
шинэ байшин барих
Build infrastructure
Build new houses

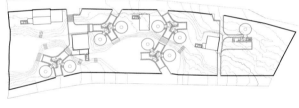

архийн тоо
No. of Households

13 👤px
13 families

3 шинэ байшин барих
Байшинг өргөтгөх
Build new houses
Extend existing houses

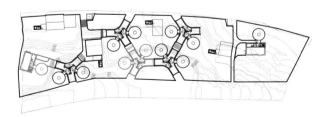

архийн тоо
No. of Households

16 👤px
16 families

УСАН ХАНГАМЖ
WATER IN

УСАН ХАНГАМЖ
WATER IN

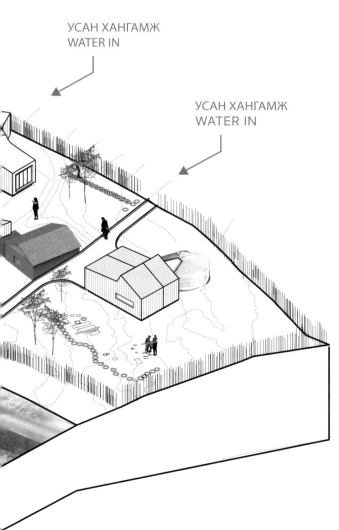

ДҮГНЭЛТ
SUMMARY

Энэ хүснэгтэд нийт бүтээгдхүүний нэр төрөл, хэрэглээ, өртөг, эрчим хүчний хэмнэлттэй бага хүүтэй зээлийн сарын төлбөр зэргийг тоймлож харуулав.

This table shows the product range, the performance, and the estimated costs and monthly repayments based on a low-interest, energy efficient mortgage.

ШИНЭ БАЙШИН NEW HOUSE	ТАЛБАЙ (M²) AREA (M²)	ӨРТӨГ (₮) COST (USD)*	ӨРТӨГ/ M2 COST/M2	U-ЗУРАГ U-VALUE	ХҮҮ, ХУГАЦАА LOAN TERMS**	САРЫН ТӨЛБӨР MONTHLY PAYMENT**
Гэр холбогч Ger Connector	28m²	5,000,000 ₮ 1,600 USD	192,300 ₮/m² 62 USD/m²	Хан Wall U=0.21 W/(m²K)	N/A	N/A
Гэр Плаг-ин (үндсэн барилга) Ger Plug-in (Core)	37.8m²	27,415,000 ₮ 8,775 USD	725,264 ₮/m² 232 USD/m²			210,630 ₮ 67 USD
Гэр Плаг-ин (өргөтгөл) Ger Plug-in (Extended)	+28m²	+24,231,000 ₮ +7,755 USD	865,390 ₮/m² 277 USD/m²	Хан Wall U=0.16 W/(m²K) Дээвэр Roof U=0.21 W/(m²K) Шал Floor U=0.21 W/(m²K)	6.16 % хүү Interest rate 180 cap months 10% Урьдчилгаа Pre-payment	185,920₮ 59 USD
Гэр Плаг-ин Ger House	39.8m²	49,694,000 ₮ 15,900 USD	1,246,330 ₮/m² 400 USD/m²			380,600₮ 122 USD
Орон сууцны байшин (гэргүй) Apartment House (no ger)	54m²	108,648,000 ₮ 34,770 USD	2,012,000 ₮/m² 644 USD/m²	Хан Wall U=0.16 W/(m²K) Дээвэр Roof U=0.21 W/(m²K) Шал Floor U=0.21 W/(m²K)	6.16 % хүү Interest rate 180 cap months 10% Урьдчилгаа Pre-payment	833,630 ₮ 267 USD
Орон сууцны байшин (гэртэй) Apartment House (with ger)	132m²	127,621,000 ₮ 40,840 USD	966,825 ₮/m² 310 USD/m²			979,200 ₮ 313 USD өрх бүр per household 326,400 ₮ 104 USD
Орон сууцны байшин (хос) Apartment House (double)	108m²	217,296,000 ₮ 69,535 USD	2,012,000 ₮/m² 644 USD/m²		N/A	N/A

ОДОО БАЙГАА БАЙШИН EXISTING HOUSE	ТАЛБАЙ (M²) AREA (M²)	ӨРТӨГ (₮) COST (USD)*	ӨРТӨГ/ M² COST/M²	U-ЗУРАГ U-VALUE	ХҮҮ, ХУГАЦАА LOAN TERMS**	САРЫН ТӨЛБӨР MONTHLY PAYMENT**
Дэд бүтцийн үндсэн хэсэг Infrastructural core	5m²	10,326,960 ₮ 3,305 USD	2,065,392 ₮/m² 661 USD/m²	Хан Wall U=0.21 W/(m²K)	3-8 % хүү Interest rate 30 cap months	8% хүү Interest rate 380,950 ₮ 122 USD
Хагас-Байшин Half-House	30m²	28,275,000 ₮ 9,048 USD	942,500 ₮/m² 302 USD/m²	Хан Wall U=0.16 W/(m²K)		8% хүү Ierest rate 1,043,017 ₮ 334 USD

ГАДНА ТАЛБАЙН ДЭД БҮТЭЦ LANDSCAPE INFRASTRUCTURE	ТАЛБАЙ (M²) AREA (M²)	ӨРТӨГ (₮) COST (USD)*	БҮТЭЦ MATERIALS
усны оролт ба усны танк Water Inlet and Tank	усны оролт ба вандан сандал Water inlet and bench 2m² 8m3 усны танк Water tank	усны оролт Water inlet 1,000,000 ₮ 320 USD усны танк Water tank 10,000,000 ₮ 3,200 USD	Усны хоолой, төмөр хүрэ, усны сав, дулаалга Water pipe, steel, water tank, insulation
дэлгүүр Shop	4.5m²	3,500,000 ₮ 1,120 USD	Тоосго, дулаалга, цонх, халхавч Brick, insulation, window, canopy
Септик сав Septic tank	1.1m³/ өрхүүд household	4,500,000 ₮ 1,440 USD өрхүүд household	Септик сав, дулаалга, хоолой Septic tank, insulation, piping
Ландшафт Landscape	0.7 га газар хүртэл up to 0.7 ha	₮25,000/m²-аас зураг төсөл, барилгын ажил from ₮ 25,000/m² for design and construction	Хан, цэцгийн сав, хашаа, явган хүний зам Retaining wall, Planters, Fencing, Pathways

* Зах зээлийн хэлбэлзлээс хамаарч үнэ өөрчлөгдөнө (валют ханш, тээврийн зардал) 2022.04-ны өдрийн ханш.
* Prices subject to change based on market fluctuations. Current rates as of April 2022.
** Зээлийн нөхцөлийг 2022 оны 4-р сарын байдлаар банкнаас авах боломжтой бүтээгдэхүүнд үндэслэсэн.
** Loan terms based on available products from banks as of April 2022. Monthly payments are indicative
   based on the stated interest rate and maximum loan term.

Our khashaa faces the
main street and we are
right opposite the water
kiosk. We see that there is
potential for us to open-up
a business here. We are very
ambitious and are planning
to build a two to three
storey complex including
a wood workshop, bakery,
and grocery shop. We also
want to add a new storey to
our current house and dig a
well in our khashaa. Me and
my husband both work in
construction. We have built
everything ourselves and so
we plan to do the same here.

Tuyatsetseg Tsedendamb

FRAME

AS

MET

WORK

HOD

This book's examination of the urban conditions in Ulaanbaatar presents an extreme case of the problems associated with contemporary urbanization in emerging economies. The learning experience of making architecture in this context has led us to reposition the role of the architect as a critical agent who both shapes and offers alternative pathways for urban transformation. This is distinct from the work of the urban planner or urban designer. It consists in strategizing how the methods of making architecture can connect back to processes of urbanization. In practice, this repositioned role entails the active design and construction of the *framework,* or conditions, in which architects work. As opposed to the traditional master plan, the term *framework* explicitly conceives a multi-scalar, dynamic, and open-ended network that the architect initiates and engages in the course of every project. Such a conceptual approach is necessary to reconcile design with the forces of contemporary urbanization, particularly in territories that are becoming urban.

DESIGNING THE URBAN IS A CONTRADICTION
The urban cannot be designed: urbanization is a process. Attempts to "master-plan" cities through parcellation, zoning laws, fixed programs, and land uses are counterproductive to the creation of urbanism, and indeed urban culture. Urban design as a discipline today has become subsumed into a subfield of static space disconnected from contemporary forces of urbanization that have reshaped the city at multiple scales. At its most banal, it has been divested of its social and political objectives and coopted by neoliberal real-estate development to ameliorate the streetscape, bring back traditional forms, and create anodyne urban niceness.[161]

It wasn't always like this. In 1956 the proclamation of the new discipline of urban design was a reaction to an identified crisis of the time: to address the widening disparity between the suburbs and the city center.[162] Urban design carved out a role for architects to rekindle the city center through civic projects and defend the urban realm from wanton large-scale development. The establishment of the first degree in urban design at Harvard in 1960,[163] fostered a link between academia and practice in order to address the shortcomings of CIAM and to engage in the struggle for an equitable and just society.[164] Over sixty years later, the conditions impacting urban development have changed. New crises have emerged, bringing with them the necessity to redefine the architect's role in shaping urban change.

URBAN PROCESSES HAVE CHANGED
The forces underpinning urbanization have changed. Globalization has reconfigured the economy as financial restructuring and information technology have transformed how we work and what we do.[165] As recent discourse around urbanization has shown, the extension of urban processes into rural territory produces landscapes that can no longer be distinguished by the binary distinction between urban and rural.[166] The modern metropolis has become unbounded, in Edward Soja's words, into distributed territories of urban agglomerations.[167]

This territorial urbanization transcends borders, creating production landscapes that operate in some cases outside of the nations in which they exist. This often strategically coordinated arrangement of actors and sites, which Keller Easterling describes as extrastatecraft,[168] is particularly pertinent to China's current model of outward externalization through urbanization. This includes its immense Belt and Road initiative, its stake in developing resource extraction and agricultural contingency in Africa, and its controversial provision of technological infrastructure across Europe.

At the same time, corporations such as Amazon, Google, and Apple operate with budgets that are larger than the GDPs of many countries. These vast corporate fortunes enable networks that link rare-earth element mining, factory production, logistics, corporate finance, and central business districts in a global web of capital accumulation. Other, less notorious companies such as BlackRock—which in 2020 had assets of $8.7 trillion—don't make or produce anything but rather generate wealth, instrumental in the continuous financing, investing, and trading that perpetuate the global finance industry.[169] These global flows of finance and trade inevitably touch down, inscribing the earth, precipitating an extensive urbanization process across the globe.

URBAN MATTER FUELS THE CLIMATE CRISIS

These underlying forces have resulted in 56 percent of the world's population living in urban centers. The rapid urbanization of the developing world is expected to increase this figure to 75 percent by 2050.[170] To meet this urgent demand, housing in developing regions is predominantly supplied by informal development. The logics of this development are governed by the pragmatics facing individual households with respect to land availability, the provision of shelter, and financial capacity. In the short term, the creation of self-built settlements, incrementally improved and constructed by residents themselves, has saved governments millions of investment dollars and shifted the responsibility of affordable housing and basic infrastructure away from the public sector. In the long term, this relentless production of urban matter is tied to the prevailing crises of the twenty-first century: climate change and income inequality.

The world's climatic future is inextricably linked to how developing regions urbanise. These areas are the locus of future population increases, with 97 percent of population growth in the next thirty years projected to occur in the developing world.[171] By 2040 developing countries will account for 67 percent of global energy consumption, with emissions increasing by five billion tons while the rest of the world plateaus or declines.[172] In such developing economies, building operations and construction account for 39 percent of carbon emissions and spent energy.[173] Each ton of carbon emissions is directly correlated to increases in global temperature that are causing accelerating rates of extreme weather such as drought, flooding, heat waves, and typhoons. Because of the substandard construction of many informal settlements, these communities are especially vulnerable to such events. Given this correlation between emerging economies, urbanization, and carbon emissions, ensuring that the developing world builds sustainably is critical to our climate future.

WE HAVE AN UNPARALLELED OPPORTUNITY

The 2016 Paris Accords offered a chance to address the disparity between developed and developing regions. The Green Climate Fund has pledged $15.6 billion from developed countries to impact sustainability in developing regions. Additionally, Environmental Sustainability Governance (ESG) assets are on track to exceed $53 trillion globally by 2025, which would account for one-third of global assets under management. Despite this, there is a lack of funds directed towards the built environment in developing countries. Energy efficient construction accounts for just 4.8 percent of climate finance annually and although the International Finance Corporation has identified that green buildings represent a $24.7 trillion investment opportunity in emerging markets by 2030, the majority of residential construction in developing countries is informally built and energy inefficient.[174] Given that each year the developing world is projected to add 3.6 billion square meters of housing to meet demand,[175] each house we build today is an opportunity to save energy that will have lasting ramifications for our climate future.

Clearly, there is both a chance and an urgent need to direct sustainable investment into the built environment. This represents a unique moment to situate a role for the architect to contribute to this pressing issue. Yet the capacity of architects to lead the design and construction of sustainable urban form in emerging regions is currently not part of the dominant discourse. Although individual projects in developing regions are noted and recognized for their social capacity to assist communities,[176] there is a distinct lack of projects that engage the potential of architecture to impact the urban scale. Furthermore, there is a disconnect between architectural practice and development agencies and funding bodies such as the World Bank, which focus on financial, rather than directly spatial, mechanisms of change. This was not always the case. As previously discussed, the example of members of Team X working alongside the United Nations Development Program demonstrates that architecture can structure urbanism and allow for adaptation and evolution by its inhabitants.[177]

THE ROLE OF THE ARCHITECT

In order to create urban fabric that does not deplete resources or further detrimental environmental conditions but instead offers an alternative development strategy for settlements and their communities to evolve over time, we must set out a position for the architect to structure the process of urban transformation in areas that are becoming urban. Architecture is the spatial setting of our lives, conditioning and enabling how we live together and forming the essential DNA of the city. Building typologies structure a city's characteristics and give rise to its spatial form. New typologies transform trajectories of settlement, changing and altering that spatial identity. Thus, architecture can impact urban transformation by way of typological change. Typological change, as I argue in chapter 3, is not limited to the formal evolution of historical precedent.[178] Rather, typologies can be generated from a situated design practice that operates under the exacting limitations of localized constraints. This work of designing and testing new typologies is what we have defined as prototyping. As a design process, it is distinct from technological prototyping—the creation of a mass-produced and universally applied singular object—as it instead produces prototypes with the capacity to adapt to the specific conditions of a site. Prototyping requires continuous testing against the particular and evolving constraints of a location. This feedback gives a prototype the potential to effect typological change. The necessary engagement with a site through prototyping initiates the construction of an ecology of practice that creates agency for a network of different stakeholders through the act of building. Our claim is that prototyping as a method must be a situated practice in order to lead to the emergence of new typologies with the potential to influence processes of urban transformation. In this way prototyping demonstrates how the architect can impact the urban scale.

Different prototypes with different functions—beyond housing—are needed to build a diverse, emerging urban realm. Prototypes that initiate cooperation and provide civic infrastructure make space for communities to define their current and future demands. These may include the recognition of collective responsibilities and the provision of communal resources that surpass individual needs. Enabling households to act based on the advantages of sharing and cooperation is a crucial step in the incremental staging of the process of becoming urban. The public realm is not something that is provided, but rather must be enabled and constructed.

Incremental urban strategies contain a diverse set of building types, are flexible and adaptable, evolve over time, and operate at multiple scales – allowing districts to evolve gradually as residents' circumstances change. Incremental development is advantageous as it harnesses the existing mechanisms found in many informal settlements. Typically, residents improve their living environments in-situ when they have the means to do so. By offering alternative design approaches that improve upon the current ad-hoc manner of such improvements, an incremental urban strategy augments existing forces of development towards collective benefit. The advantages of applying this approach in existing settlements include maintaining existing neighborhoods and community networks, keeping residents close to their jobs, and building upon inhabitants' original investments in their land or their property. In essence, an incremental urban strategy is one that works through the process of prototyping, is staged over time, and works with the embedded logics of a specific site.

BUILDING THE FRAMEWORK
The process of designing and deploying prototypes within an incremental strategy can be understood as a framework. This framework is an approach and method, but it is also constructed through doing. Unlike some frameworks that are understood as a matrix of guidelines, building a framework is an active process, developed and led by the architect's roles of situating a project in its site and among its stakeholders, and of deploying prototypes in an incremental strategy. That is to say, *frameworking* is a methodology—an alternative to the limitations of the master plan to enact change.

*Since I have a lot of kids,
I wish to live somewhere big.
Area of at least 80m² and two
storys. Living in my mother's
land is difficult, I want to
have something of my own,
in my own khashaa I would
plant trees and flowers.
Working together with my
neighbors and actually
achieving something is good.*

Erdenechimeg Ishjamts

Current approaches to master-planning are proving ineffective in sites that are in the process of becoming urban, as they require political and economic certainty that is often not present. The demise of the public sector in many free-market economies makes the implementation of master plans dependent on neoliberal mechanisms and financial tools. Despite the intentions of positioning profit incentives for development projects in hopes to stimulate the economy and create jobs, relying on the private sector to deliver master plans means that often the most vulnerable communities are overlooked, and that social and civic infrastructure, such as community, educational, and recreational spaces, are not prioritized. In the case of Mongolia, like many emerging economies, the lack of economic and political stability and the uncertainty of guaranteed profit for the private sector has meant that master plans are unrealizable, impotent, and obsolete. It is in this gap, in places where the formal planning operations of the master plan are simply not working, that the alternative method of building the framework operates most effectively and is needed most urgently.

WHAT IS THE FRAMEWORK?

Certain conceptual themes underpin the basis of the framework. For us as architects, these themes shape criteria to guide our method of practice. The following can be understood as an expression of the ideas of an architect piecing together coherent approaches to practice rather than a definitive theory of architecture.

THE FRAMEWORK IS A MULTI-SCALAR ECOLOGY

Thinking about how architecture and the urban inform each other requires multiple scales to be considered at the same time. The CIAM Grid of 1948 was a mechanism to structure how different scales can impact the urban, from the master plan to the building. However, this categorization risks becoming reductive to solely the consideration of built form as opposed to thinking of the influence of other dynamics on urban development. Team X recognised this limitation in their counterproposal that foregrounded the creation of urban habitats, the Re-identification Grid of 1953.[179] This matrix introduced more qualitative than quantitative information, made explicit through the use of Nigel Henderson's photographs of everyday settings in London's East End. The concept of the framework builds on this legacy, focusing on the relationships between elements in the system. The framework can be considered as an ecology as it is constructed out of the dynamics between different components at different scales within a network of actors generating numerous inputs, outputs, and feedback loops.

THE FRAMEWORK IS DYNAMIC

Frameworks are tied to contexts that are in flux, transitioning from one state to another. By considering the time-based change of multiple components undergoing different speeds of transformation, a nonlinear understanding of urban development can be conceived. This means thinking about urban development not just as different sequential phases but as a dynamic process.[180] The analysis of a site needs to deploy methods that can reveal the underlying forces and pressures that shape larger urban dynamics. A context can be changed by harnessing these existing forces or by actions taken across the different scales that shape and alter the form of urban transformation.

THE FRAMEWORK CONTAINS OUTLIERS AND MISFITS

Anomalies can reveal emergent urban phenomena, exhibiting new tendencies that can influence trends in urban development. In my hometown of Manchester, the Hulme Crescents was presented in the press as an abject failure of public housing—'a crime riddled concrete jungle'—yet it is also mythologized as the source of Manchester's music scene and a trigger for its later cultural renaissance.[181] Outliers like these resist conventional forms of planning and often bypass current trends and political or economic motivations behind urban restructuring.

Matthias Ungers' 1977 project for the *City in the City* operated similarly against an understanding of the city as a singular whole, instead advocating for the creation of islands of extreme identities that would exist in contradiction to their adjacent context.[182] The resulting contrasts between intense specificity and generic ubiquity, country and city, the past and its unfolding future, describe how the initiation of such dialectical moments can be a productive driver of the city's development. In this way, anomalies and misfits, residual spaces and leftovers, are opportunities to catalyse alternative models of urban change.

THE FRAMEWORK IS OPEN-ENDED

The framework is not overly deterministic. Rather, it steers the process of urbanization through both that which can be controlled and that which remains uncontrolled. Strategically, this means designing structures that set out how future development occurs yet allow for other actors to participate in the construction process. For example, the clarity of the organizational diagram of a prototype is a key aspect that needs to be retained, whereas material choice or room layout is something that can be determined by residents.

The framework is not as open ended in intention as, for example, the Non-Plan of Cedric Price[183] but rather tries to build upon concepts such as Fumihiko Maki's Master form[184] and Andrea Branzi's Weak Urbanism,[185] which involve ideas of incompleteness, adaptation, and time-based change. A combination of loose and tight urban models can generate a productive tension that stimulates diversity and variation. Contrasting fixed or more permanent stable entities with temporary or ephemeral programs and land uses can lead to a diverse set of urban experiences and spatial outcomes.

THE FRAMEWORK REPOSITIONS THE ROLE OF THE ARCHITECT

Building the framework, the architect's position is continually redefined within a network of stakeholders. In the process of making spaces to trigger and enable new programs, infrastructures, or social relationships, the role of the architect extends beyond the typical client-architect relationship. To build the framework the architect cannot be subservient to a singular client with a given program and set budget. Instead, the architect must invent the program, design the constraints, and, sometimes, find the money. In effect, the architect is also entrepreneur, investor, community activator, policy advisor, technician, and builder. This means setting up the conditions for architecture to take place as much as making the architecture itself.

FRAMEWORK AS METHOD

The five conceptual points above illustrate how the framework is a way of thinking that differs from the master plan and offers an alternative role for the architect in shaping urban processes. The framework is also a method, a way of working, and it is structured as follows:

SITUATING

Site specificity is critical to understanding the underlying urban dynamics that shape processes of urban change. Considering the site as a multi-scalar ecology, as a dynamic system, affects how we analyze the city. This involves drawing urban change at multiple scales, which can include drone-mapping a settlement or documenting the alteration of plots and structures made by residents. In Ulaanbaatar, our observations that most residents keep their ger even after they build a house and of the incremental steps taken by residents to improve their dwellings, were key in shaping our design and strategic approach, revealing how urban change was occurring at the scale of the individual plot and its concurrent impact on broader settlement growth.

PROTOTYPING

Prototyping is a situated practice subject to the exacting constraints of a location, including climatic, material, construction, and financial factors. Prototyping is an iterative process, requiring feedback from residents, technical experts, development agencies, and financial institutions, as well as the performance evaluation of the pilot projects themselves. The act of building prototypes results in specific knowledge that, in turn, can inform a strategic approach. Prototyping aims to initiate typological change in order to shift the trajectory of urban development but, crucially, it also activates and initiates agency for a network of stakeholders. Prototyping can be considered agile—in project management terminology—as it operates with a focused project as an increment of a whole, reflecting a comparatively low risk compared to the high investment costs necessary for top-down planning implementation.

Requiring iteration, constant improvement, and upgrading, successful prototypes nonetheless have the potential to drive large scale impact through typological change.

INCREMENTAL STRATEGY
Most informal settlements grow incrementally as residents' lives change and population increases. Incremental develop-ment therefore is no linear but involves multiple components undergoing different speeds of transformation. By coopting the existing dynamics of informal settlements into a strategic approach, incremental strategies create mechanisms for upgrading that work in-situ in respone to different demands. Incremental planning provides a structured route through which residents can improve their living conditions gradually according to shared collective goals and responsibilities. As individual needs extend to community needs, different prototypes can address the variety of programs that relate to civic infrastructure. The argument for incrementality to off-load a proportion of costs to residents themselves without large-scale investment from the public sector is only beneficial if the form of development prioritizes more sustainable forms of growth. Otherwise, haphazard development leads to the creation of detrimental environmental conditions. Ideally, the financial model includes the involvement of the public sector or international development agencies to support those aspects that remain economically out of reach for residents. This may be through the provision of infrastructure or subsidized loan agreements to nudge the development process towards more holistic objectives. An incremental plan must be adaptable to different financial models and robust enough not to rely on a single source of funding. It needs to include clear stages of development that demonstrate how residents can improve their living conditions over time, with or without top-down support.

BECOMING URBAN
Developing regions with emerging economies are undergoing rapid urbanization. With this, the impacts of climate change and the wealth gap between the rich and poor are becoming ever more acute. The predominant perspective from the developed world is of a devolved responsibility, that this only happens in the elsewhere. As architects, we have expertise in making spaces that can enable rather than encumber. Problem-solving might be a sullied term from the distorted modernism of the 60s and 70s, yet the exemplary ambitions of Team X started a project where architects were emboldened to be at the frontline of decision making and action planning, and were inventors of new architectures that offered solutions to the crises of their time. Today, the deterioration of the public sector and the reliance on private capital means that the conditions for development have drastically changed. This book does not advocate for a lost political ideology but merely that architecture is a social act. As the dynamics of urban expansion unfold, the framework offers a method to engage these emerging challenges through design.

The Mongolian project is an
ecology of practice.

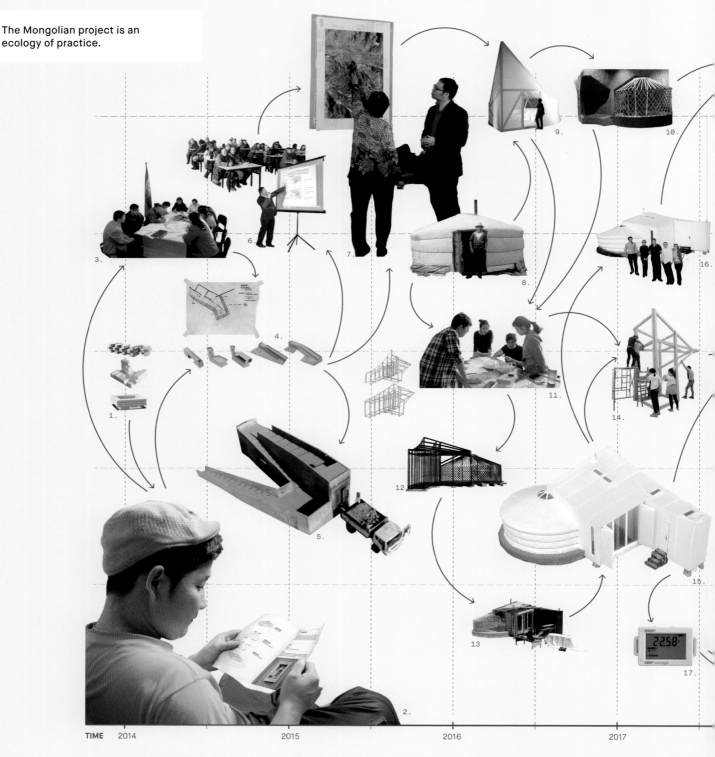

TIME   2014   2015   2016   2017

1. Initial investigation of issues and developing a suitcase of ideas
2. Meeting local residents and presenting ideas
3. Meetings and presentations with stakeholders such as The Asia Foundation, Khoroo Governors, and Mayor's Office
4. Design development of three Waste Collection Points
5. Completion of Waste Collection Point
6. Community engagement and education hosted by khoroo office
7. Community workshop to identify issues and test ideas with Gerhub
8. Conducting household visits and interviews

9. Prototyping though exhibition - Venice Biennale 2016
10. Prototyping though exhibition - Design Museum 2016
11. Ger Plug-In design development and student workshops
12. 1:1 Structural prototype of Ger Plug-In built with students
13. Construction of Ger Plug-In
14. Modular prototyping student workshop with students
15. Completion of Ger Plug-In
16. Stakeholder open house with banks, ngos, government, other development agencies.
17. In-use monitoring and data collection of Ger Plug-In
18. Prototyping through exhibition - Common Good 2018
19. Design development of Ger Innovation Hub

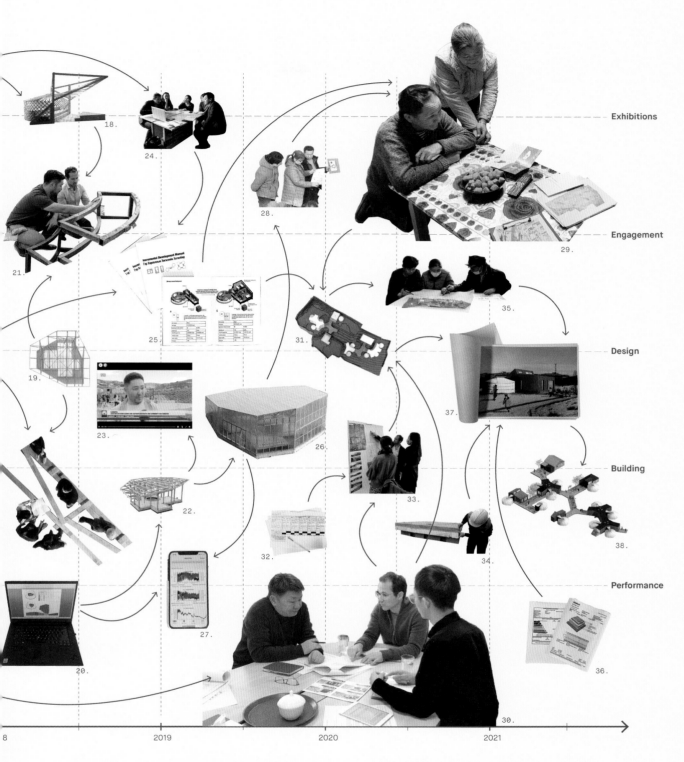

18.
24.
28.
21.
25.
19.
23.
26.
22.
31.
35.
37.
33.
20.
27.
32.
34.
38.
36.
30.

Exhibitions

Engagement
29.

Design

Building

Performance

8   2019   2020   2021

20. Environmental modelling of Ger Innovation Hub
21. Project meetings with key stakeholder NGOs and involvement of local carpenters and mudbrick manufacturer
22. Construction of Ger Innovation Hub and student workshop
23. Ecotown Playground concept design and independent construction
24. Meetings with Mongolian Sustainable Finance Corporation and XacBank
25. Ger Plug-In 2.0 development
26. Ger Innovation Hub Completion
27. Data logging and analysis for the Ger Innovation Hub
28. Ger Innovation Hub soft opening and community workshop

29. Identifying and interviewing families for the 4-Plot Development Project
30. Meeting with GIZ for Ger Plug-In 2.0 performance evaluation
31. 4-Plot Development design development
32. Baseline study of selected households.
33. Engagement of environmental engineers
34. Engagement of prefabricated concrete factory
35. Testing ideas and getting feedback from research clusters
36. Engagement with GIZ and banks to develop financial strategy
37. Creation of Incremental Development Manual
38. Implementation of housing prototypes

ENDNOTES

BECOMING URBAN

1. M. Fernandez-Gimenez, "Sustaining the Steppes: A Geographical History of Pastoral Land Use in Mongolia," *Geographical Review,* Vol. 90, No. 3, 1999, p326.
2. Figure derived from data found in the "2020 Population and Housing Census of Mongolia, National Report" (National Statistics Office of Mongolia, 2020), Table 2.3: Population growth in aimags and the capital by percentage, 1989–2000, 2000–2010, 2010–2020, and Table 2.5: Population in aimags ad the capital, by sex, and sex ratio, 2010, 2020.
3. The original area of Ulaanbaatar was around 130 km² (50.2 mile²) and has grown to over 4,700 km² (1814.7 mile²) in 2020. See Takuya Kamata, James Reichert, Tumentsogt Tsevegmid, Yoonhee Kim, and Brett Sedgewick. "Managing Urban Expansion in Mongolia." (World Bank, Washington, DC. License: Creative Commons Attribution CC BY 3.0 IGO. 2010) and National Statistics Office Mongolia, Mongolian Statistical Information Service, "Administrative and territorial units by region, aimags, and the Capital city," 2020.
4. Hannah Ritchie and Max Roser, 2018. "Urbanization." OurWorldInData.org. https://ourworldindata.org/urbanization.
5. The Three Gorges Dam Project resettled 1.13 million people in 1998 - Brooke Wilmsen & Andrew van Hulten, 2017. Following resettled people over time: the value of longitudinal data collection for understanding the livelihood impacts of the Three Gorges Dam, China, *Impact Assessment and Project Appraisal*, 35:1, 94–105, https://doi.10.1080/1 461517.2016.1271542.
6. Sixteen million people were resettled between 2016 and 2020. S. Rogers, J. Li, K. Lo, H. Guo, C. Li. *China's rapidly evolving practice of poverty resettlement: Moving millions to eliminate poverty*. Dev Policy Rev. 2020; 38: 541–554. https://doi.org/10.1111/dpr.12435.
7. Ministry of Housing, 2020. Live tables on social housing sales. https://www.gov.uk/government/statistical-data-sets/live-tables-on-social-housing-sales#social-housing-sales.
8. W. Lewis, January 16, 2020. Proportion of income to rent hits 75 percent in parts of England. https://www.propertyreporter.co.uk/landlords/proportion-of-income-to-rent-hits-75-in-parts-of-england.html#:~:text=Today%2C%20the%20proportion%20of%20income,in%20the%20last%2020%20years.
9. J. Woetzel, S. Ram, J. Mischke, N. Garemo, S. Sankhe, 2014. "A Blueprint for Addressing the Global Affordable Housing Challenge," McKinsey Global Institute, https://www.mckinsey.com/~/media/mckinsey/featured%20insights/urbanization/tackling%20the%20worlds%20affordable%20housing%20challenge/mgi_affordable_housing_full%20report_october%202014.pdf.
10. Hannah Ritchie and Max Roser, 2018. "Urbanization." https://ourworldindata.org/urbanization.
11. Celestine Bohelen, 2019. "Behind the Curtain of Post Soviet Regimes", *New York Times,* October 16, 2019. https://www.nytimes.com/2019/10/16/opinion/post-soviet-regime-elections.html.
12. Peter Stein, "Mongolia Seeks Investors for Coal Deposit" *Wall Street Journal,* December 29, 2010.
13. H. Gloystein, 2016. "Coal prices fall to 12-year lows as China, India join demand slowdown."*Reuters.* https://www.reuters.com/article/coal-prices-idINKCN0QOO5F20150819
14. Neil Brenner, 2014. Implosions/explosions: towards a study of planetary urbanization. https://search.ebscohost.com/login.aspx?direct=true&scope=site&db=nlebk&db=nlabk&AN=1449180.
15. OECD/SWAC, 2020. *Africa's Urbanization Dynamics 2020: Africapolis, Mapping a New Urban Geography*, West African Studies, *OECD Publishing,* Paris, https://doi.org/10.1787/b6bccb81-en
16. J. Bolchover, and J. Lin. Rural *Urban Framework: Transforming the Chinese Countryside*. Basel: Birkhäuser Verlag Gmbh, 2014. Print.
17. Hong Kong Director of Health, 2021. "Isolation order for Number 20, 22, 24 and 26 Reclamation Street, Yau Ma Tei, Kowloon", Press Release, Friday January 215, 2021. Available at https://www.info.gov.hk/gia/general/202101/15/P2021011500793.htm
18. "Fewer than half of those with a household income of less than £15,000 lived close to green space but 63 percent of those with a household income of more than £35,000 could find green space within five minutes" walk of their home." Patrick Barkham, 2020. "Poorer People and Ethnic Minorities Live Further from UK Green Spaces—study", The Guardian, September 16, 2020. https://www.theguardian.com/inequality/2020/sep/16/poorer-uk-households-have-less-access-to-green-spaces-study
19. United Nations, World Urbanization Prospects, 2021, United Nations Department of Economic and Social Affairs, https://www.un.org/en/development/desa/population/publications/database/index.asp.
20. Le Corbusier, Jean-Louis Cohen, and John Goodman. *Toward an Architecture*. Los Angeles, Calif: Getty Research Institute, 2007.
21. See for example: Forman, F., Cruz, T., *Top Down/Bottom Up: The Political and Architectural Practice of Estudio Teddy Cruz + Forman*. Hatje Cantz Verlag, Berlin, 2017; Marc Angélil, and Charlotte Malterre-Barthes. *Housing Cairo: The Informal Response*. Berlin: Ruby Press, 2016. Print. Jessica Bridger, and Christian Werthmann. *Metropolis Nonformal*. Oro Editions, 2016. Print. Alfredo Brillembourg, Kristin Feireiss, and Hubert Klumpner. *Informal City: Caracas Case; Urban Think Tank*. 2005. Print.
22. A. Pedret, 2013. Team 10: An Archival History (1st ed.). Routledge
23. P. Land, 2021. *The Experimental Housing Project* (PREVI), *Lima - Design and Technology in a New Neighborhood* (1st ed.). University of Los Andes in Bogota (Uniandes).
24. Anthony Vidler and James Stirling. 2010. *James Frazer Stirling: notes from the archive*. [Montréal]: Canadian Center for Architecture. P. 166.
25. J. F. C. Turner, 1977. *Housing by People*. Pantheon.
26. UN Habitat, 2020. "New Urban Agenda". https://unhabitat.org/the-new-urban-agenda-illustrated
27. "Population Living in Slums." Urban Indicators Database, Un Habitat, May 12, 2020. https://data.unhabitat.org/datasets/52c52084f31a403397e2c3bbee37f378

SETTLING THE NOMADS

NOMADIC LIFE

28. Asian Development Bank, "Project Result/Case Study: Building affordable, green houses in Mongolia's ger districts," Asian Development Bank. May 2022. https://www.adb.org/results/building-affordable-greenhouses-mongolia-s-ger-districts.
29. According to government statistics, Ulaanbaatar experienced an in-migration of 72,887 between 2015 and 2020. National Statistics Office of Mongolia, 2020 Population and Housing Census of Mongolia, National Report, National Statistics Office, Ulaanbaatar, 2020. Accessed May 2022. https://1212.mn/BookLibraryDownload.ashx?url=Census2020_Main_report_Eng.pdf&ln=En
30. "Mongolia Voluntary National Report 2019," Sustainable Development, United Nations, 2019, https://sustainabledevelopment.un.org/content/documents/23342MONGOLIA_VOLUNTARY_NATIONAL_REVIEW_REPORT_2019.pdf
31. National Statistics Office of Mongolia, 2020 Population and Housing Census of Mongolia, National Report, National Statistics Office, Ulaanbaatar, 2020, Accessed May 2022, https://1212.mn/BookLibraryDownload.ashx?url=Census2020_Main_report_Eng.pdf&ln=En

NOMADIC LIFE

32. Ole Bruun, and Li Narangoa, eds. *Mongols from Country to City: Floating Boundaries, Pastoralism and City Life in the Mongol Lands*. Copenhagen: NIAS Press, 2006.
33. The following words and phrases exist: niited tushiglesen amidral (нийтэд түшиглэсэн амьдрал), living with reliance on a group of people; hamtiin negdel (хамтын нэгдэл), a grouping of people; and hamt olon (хамт олон), a group of people that you are a part of. However, there is no word that translates directly as community. This observation was brought to light in conversation with Badruun Gardi, CEO of the NGO GerHub. Badruun discussed that despite the lexical gap, with people today living together in close proximity in the ger districts, there is an urgent need for a place for them to come together for collective activities.
34. M. Fernandez-Gimenez, "Sustaining the Steppes: A Geographical History of Pastoral Land Use in Mongolia," Geographical Review, vol. 90, no. 3, 1999, p319.
35. Alicia Campi, "The Rise of Cities in Nomadic Mongolia." In Mongols from Country to City, Bruun and Narangoa, eds.
36. M. Fernandez-Gimenez, "Sustaining the Steppes: A Geographical History of Pastoral Land Use in Mongolia," Geographical Review, vol. 90, no. 3, 1999, p320.
37. M.C. Goldstein and C.M. Beal, *The Changing World of Mongolia's Nomads*, Los Angeles, University of California Press, 1994, p18.
38. B. Shiréndèv, W. Brown, U. Onon, & Harvard University. East Asian Research Center. *History of the Mongolian People's Republic* (Harvard East Asian monographs; 65). Cambridge, Mass.: East Asian Research Center, Harvard University, 1976.
39. Kaplonski, Christopher. "Prelude to Violence: Show Trials and State Power in 1930s Mongolia." American Ethnologist 35, no. 2, 2008: 321–37. Accessed April 9, 2021. http://www.jstor.org/stable/27667492.
40. Baabar, Kaplonski, & Kaplonski, C. Twentieth century Mongolia. Cambridge: White Horse Press, 1999.
41. Bawden, C. The modern history of Mongolia (2nd ed.] ed., KPI paperbacks). London ; New York: Kegan Paul International, 1989.
42. Worden, R., Savada, A., & Library of Congress. Federal Research Division, 1991. Mongolia, a country study (2nd ed., Area handbook series). Washington, D.C.: Federal Research Division, Library of Congress: For sale by the Supt. of Docs., U.S. G.P.O., 1991.
43. David Sneath. *The Rural and the Urban in Pastoral Mongolia. In Mongolia Remade*. Amsterdam University Press, 2018, p. 57.
44. Bruun and Narangoa, eds. *Mongols from Country to City*.

45. International Federation of Red Cross and Red Crescent Societies, "Mongolia: Dzud Early Action Protocol Summary", 2020. Online. https://reliefweb.int/sites/reliefweb.int/files/resources/EAP2020MN02_summary.pdf

46. Matthias Helble, Hal Hill, and Declan Magee. *Mongolia's Economic Prospects: Resource-rich and Landlocked between Two Giants.* Asian Development Bank, 2020, p.73. Internet resource.

47. "Mongolia: Transactions with the Fund," International Monetary Fund, April 30 2021. https://www.imf.org/external/np/fin/tad/extrans1.aspx?memberKey1=675&endDate=2099-12-31&finposition_flag=YES

48. "Population of Mongolia, " 1212, Mongolian Statistical Information Service, 2021. https://www.1212.mn/Stat.aspx?LIST_ID=976_L03&type=tables.

49. Takuya Kamata et al. *Mongolia: Enhancing Policies and Practices for Ger Area Development in Ulaanbaatar.* Herndon, VA, USA: World Bank Publications, 2010.

URBAN LIFE

50. Alicia Campi, "The Rise of Cities in Nomadic Mongolia" in *Mongols: From Country to City Floating Boundaries, Pastorialism and City Life in the Mongol Lands.* Ole Bruun and Li Narangoa. Eds. NIAS Press. 2006.

51. C.R. Bawden, *The Modern History of Mongolia,* 2nd ed. London: Kegan Paul International, 1989.

52. For example, Dambadorj in 1928. See B. Batbaatar,1999, *History of Mongolia,* D. Suhjargalmaa et al., Cambridge, University of Cambridge, p287.

53. Alicia Campi, "The Rise of Cities in Nomadic Mongolia" in *Mongols: From Country to City Floating Boundaries, Pastorialism and City Life in the Mongol Lands.* Ole Bruun and Li Narangoa. Eds. NIAS Press. 2006.

54. Chinbat Badamdorj, 2004 "Changes in the Internal Structure of Ulaanbaatar, Mongolia." Scientific Annual of Korea Mongolian Economic Association 14 (1): 1–15.

55. Alexander C Diener, and Joshua Hagen, "City of felt and concrete: Negotiating cultural hybridity in Mongolia's capital of Ulaanbaatar." Nationalities Papers, 2013 Vol 41, No.4, 622–650.

56. Byambadorj, Tseregmaa, Marco Amati, and Kristian J Ruming, 2011, "Twenty-first Century Nomadic City: Ger Districts and Barriers to the Implementation of the Ulaanbaatar City Master Plan." Asia Pacific Viewpoint 52, no. 2, pp. 171.

57. A. C. Diener, and J. Hagen, 2015. *From socialist to post-socialist cities: cultural politics of architecture, urban planning, and identity in Eurasia,* Routledge, Oxfordshire.

58. Ibid.

59. Byambadorj, Tseregmaa, Marco Amati, and Kristian J Ruming. 2011 "Twenty-first Century Nomadic City: Ger Districts and Barriers to the Implementation of the Ulaanbaatar City Master Plan." Asia Pacific Viewpoint 52, no. 2, pp. 171.

60. World Bank Group, 2018. *"Mongolia Systematic Country Diagnostic".* World Bank, Washington, DC. © World Bank. https://openknowledge.worldbank.org/handle/10986/30973.

61. Turquoise Hill, "2020 Annual Report", Turquoise Hill Ltd, pp. 93.

62. Alistair Macdonald, 2021. "Rio Tinto Mismanagement Caused Mongolia Copper Mine's Woes, Report Says". The Wall Street Journal. https://www.wsj.com/articles/rio-tinto-mismanagement-caused-mongolia-copper-mines-woes-report-says-11628503201.

63. World Bank Group, 2018,*"Mongolia Systematic Country Diagnostic".* World Bank, Washington, DC. https://openknowledge.worldbank.org/handle/10986/30973 License: CC BY 3.0 IGO.

64. William Turner, 2015, Affordable Housing and Ger Area Redevelopment in Ulaanbaatar, MAD Investment Solutions. http://www.madurb.com/wp-content/uploads/2015/11/Affordable-Housing-and-Ger-Area-Redevelopment-in-Ulaanbaatar.pdf.

65. Ibid.

66. E. Ishjamts, 2016. Interview by Duulgaan Bayasgalan, "Fear and Love: Reactions to a Complex World," November 24, 2016.

GER DISTRICT LIFE

67. Interview with Zul-Erdene Sharavjamts (Zulaa) conducted by author on December 5 2017.

68. Asian Development Bank, 2020 "Building affordable, green houses in Mongolia's ger districts," Asian Development Bank, Manilla. https://www.adb.org/results/building-affordable-greenhouses-mongolia-s-ger-districts.

69. T. Kamata, J. Reichert, T. Tsevegmid, Y. Kim, B. Sedgewick, 2010, "Enhancing Policies and Practices for Ger Area Development in Ulaanbaatar" (English). Washington, D.C. : World Bank Group. https://documents.worldbank.org/pt/publication/documents-reports/documentdetail/288141468061498905/mongolia-enhancing-policies-and-practices-for-ger-area-development-in-ulaanbaatar.

70. A. Munkhzul, 2020, "First Subprogram on Reducing Soil Pollution in Ulaanbaatar Being Developed", Montsame, Ulaanbaatar. August 26, 2020. https://montsame.mn/en/read/234591.

71. J. Hincks, 2018, "Life in the Most Polluted Capital in the World", Time Magazine, March 23, 2018. https://time.com/longform/ulan-bator-mongolia-most-polluted-capital/.

72. National Agency for Meteorology and Environmental Monitoring, and Air Quality, 2021, "Ulaanbaatar Air Pollution: Real-Time Air Quality Index," National Agency for Meteorology and Environmental Monitoring Department, Capital City, Ulaanbaatar, Mongolia. aqicn.org/city/ulaanbaatar/mnb.

73. National Center for Public Health and UNICEF, 2018. "Mongolia's Air Pollution Crisis: A call to action to protect children's health," National Center for Public Health, Ulaanbaatar, Mongolia, 2018, Accessed January 25, 2021.

74. World Bank, Enhancing Policies and Practices for Ger Area Development in Ulaanbaatar, 9.

75. National Statistics Office, 2020, "Resident Population In Mongolia," by Khoroo, Urban and Rural, National Statistics Office, Ulaanbaatar. https://en.nso.mn.

76. Census and Statistics Department, 2016, "Thematic Household Survey Report No. 60: Housing conditions of sub-divided units in Hong Kong," Census and Statistics Department, Hong Kong Administrative Region. March 2016. https://www.censtatd.gov.hk/en/press_release_detail.html?id=3965.

77. Many case studies of informal slums have been documented such as those in Brazil (Angélil, Hehl, 2011), Thailand (Johnson, Or, 2010), South Africa (Patel, 2013), Turkey (Arefi, 2011), India (Abelson, 1996). A particularly pertinent example is Janice Perlman's seminal work on the favelas of Brazil, extensively studying the effects of violence, exclusion, and increased levels of "marginality" occurring in Rio de Janeiro, Perlman, 2011.

78. J. Bolchover, and J. Lin, 2014, *Rural Urban Framework: Transforming the Chinese Countryside.* De Gruyter, Berlin, Print.

79. In depth interviews with 19 residents from Chingeltei-16 and Sukhbaatar-16 were conducted in November 2016.

80. JICA, 2020, Ulaanbaatar City Master Planning 2030. Part II: City Master Planning 2030, Japan International Cooperation Agency, Tokyo, Japan, https://openjicareport.jica.go.jp/pdf/11937158_02.pdf.

81. Economic Research Institute, 2013, "An Economic Impact Assessment Of The Committed Chinggis Bond Allocation," Economic Research Institute, Ulaanbaatar, Mongolia, 2013. http://www.eri.mn/research/345-ewohxidw.

82. JICA, Ulaanbaatar City Master Planning 2030.

83. ADB. 2020, "Asian Development Bank and Mongolia: Fact Sheet" Asian Development Bank. Manilla, Phillipines.

84. Asia Development Bank, 2018, "Mongolia: Ulaanbaatar Green Affordable Housing and Resilient Urban Renewal Sector Project: Voluntary Land Swapping Plan," Asia Development Bank, Manilla, Phillipines, Viewed August 2021, https://www.adb.org/sites/default/files/linked-documents/49169-002-sd-01.pdf.

85. Koyanagi, K 2017, "Battered Mongolia faces make-or-break moment", Nikkei Asian Review, Viewed August 2021, https://asia.nikkei.com/Economy/Battered-Mongolia-faces-make-or-break-moment.

86. XacBank Eco-Banking team, 2018. Interview by Joshua Bolchover, November 2018 .

87. Correspondence with Batbold Sukhbaatar, Executive Director of Erel Group, May 28, 2021.

PROTOTYPING

BUILDING AS RESEARCH

88. See J. Durand, 2000. *Precis of the lectures on architecture; with graphic portion of the lectures on architecture* (Texts & documents). Los Angeles, Calif.: Getty Research Institute.

89. Rafael Moneo, 1978. On Typology, *Oppositions 13.*

90. Aldo Rossi, 2007. *The Architecture of the City.* Cambridge, Mass.: MIT Press.

91. Le Corbusier, 1986. *Towards a new architecture.* New York: Dover.

92. This pursuit is well documented in the exhibition and publication "Home Delivery: Fabricating the Modern Dwelling." See Bergdoll, Barry, Peter. Christensen, Ron. Broadhurst, and Museum of Modern Art, 2008. *Home Delivery: Fabricating the Modern Dwelling.* New York: Museum of Modern Art.

93. G. Herbert, 1984. *The dream of the factory-made house: Walter Gropius and Konrad Wachsmann.* Cambridge, Mass.: MIT Press.

94. Aureli, Pier Vittorio, 2014. "The Dom-Ino Problem: Questioning the Architecture of Domestic Space." Log, no. 30, Anyone Corporation. pp. 153–68, http://www.jstor.org/stable/43631744.

95. Aureli argues that the mechanism of construction is a "subtle form of social engineering." The creation of a local labor force and access to home ownership appeasing residents and taming the possibility of social unrest while still linking profits of construction materials back to larger corporate structures.

96. Peter Eisenman, 1979. *Aspects of Modernism: Maison Dom-ino and the Self-Referential Sign in Architecture.* Oppositions 15/16 (Winter/Spring 1979): 118–28.

97. J. Bolchover, and J. Lin, 2014. *Rural Urban Framework: Transforming the Chinese countryside.* Basel: Birkhäuser Verlag gmbh.

98. NBSC. *China Statistical Yearbook 2020,* 2020. China Statistics Press: Beijing, China.

99. A. Martins, and J. Saavedra Farias, 2019. *Inclusive sustainability within favela upgrading and incremental housing: The case of Rocinha in Rio de Janeiro.* Sustainable

Development (Bradford, West Yorkshire, England), 27(2), 205–213.

100. F. Miraftab, and N. Kudva, 2015. *Cities of the global South reader* (Routledge urban reader series). Abingdon, Oxon ; New York, NY: Routledge.

101. U. Rao, 2010. *Making the Global City: Urban Citizenship at the Margins of Delhi*. Ethnos, 75(4), 402–424.

102. For example, the George Sturges House, 1939, compared to the Lloyd Lewis House, 1939. See Pfeiffer, Bruce Brooks., and Yukio Futagawa. *Frank Lloyd Wright: Usonian Houses*. GA Traveler; 005. Tokyo: A.D.A Edita, 2002.

103. For example, the Gerald and Beverley Tonkens House, 1954, or the Toufic H. Kalil House, 1955. See Morse-Fortier, J. Leonard, 1994, From "Frank Lloyd Wright's Usonian Automatic Building System: Lessons and Limitations in a Lost Paradigm." Journal of Architectural and Planning Research, vol. 11, no. 4, Locke Science Publishing Company, Inc. pp. 274–93, http://www.jstor.org/stable/43029134.

104. J. Bolchover, and J. Lin, *Rural Urban Framework: Transforming the Chinese Countryside*, Birkhauser, Basel, October 2013.

PRODUCTIVE FAILURE

105. "Settling the Nomads" in Reporting from the Front curated by Alejandro Aravena at la Biennale di Venezia, Venice, May 28–November 27, 2016.

106. "City of Nomads" in Fear and Love: Reactions to a Complex World curated by Justin Mcguirk at The Design Museum, London, November 24–April 27, 2017.

107. "Ger Community Hub" in Common Good, Museum for Applied Arts and Sciences (MAAS), Sydney, March 2–December 2, 2018.

ENABLING COMMUNITY

108. Khaliun Bayartsogt (Agence France-Presse), "Kindergarten lottery means children miss out on early education in Mongolia", September 29, 2017. https://theirworld.org/news/mongolia-kindergarten-crisis-lottery-for-places.

109. The demand for kindergartens and childcare in Songino Khairkhan 43 was evidenced in our interview with the district leader on November 21, 2019, who described it as a persistent issue that they have been petitioning to the District Office to resolve for many years as the current kindergarten is oversubscribed.

110. Jamie Chu, "Breathing new life: Tulou tower and plug-in, Lantian village, China by Rural Urban Framework + University of Hong Kong", The Architectural Review, Issue 1467, New Into Old, EMAP Publishing Ltd, United Kingdom, December 2019.

111. Francesco Garutti, "From within an ecology of practice", The Things Around Us:51N4E and Rural Urban Framework, edited by Francesco Garutti, Canadian Center for Architecture, Montreal, 2021.

112. "Incremental Development Manual: The Ger Innovation Hub, Mongolia", 2020 AIA/ACSA Intersections Research Conference: CARBON, September 30 to October 2, 2020, Virtual Conference.

113. The cost of the building in 2019 was $67,500 for 160 square meters, or $420 per square meter. The Mongolian standard for house construction varies from $630 per square meter for a well-insulated house with infrastructure to a standard baishin at $100 per square meter.

114. "The Things Around Us: 51N4E and Rural Urban Framework", The Canadian Center for Architecture, Montreal, September 16 2020-March 21 2021.

115. See Joshua Bolchover and Peter Hasdell,

Border Ecologies: Hong Kong's Mainland Frontier, Birkhauser, Basel, 2017.

PLUG-IN: TRANSFORMING AND UPGRADING

116. Involving a sample of 59 households, surveys were conducted by the Asia Foundation between November 2019 and January 2020, with the final report titled "Incremental Development Manual: Demonstrating a Model for Ger District Upgrading" project, Market Research Report", completed in February 2020.

117. This is consistent with findings from other studies conducted by the World Bank. See Singh, Gayatri. "Urban Poverty In Ulaanbaatar: Understanding the Dimensions and Addressing the Challenges." World Bank. Washington DC. License: Creative Commons Attribution CC BY 3.0 IGO. 2017.

118. From the sample of the residents earning above the median income of ₮1,050,000 ($382) per month, 9 lived in gers and 12 lived in houses, while of those in the lower income levels, 9 lived in gers and 10 in houses. The Asia Foundation, 2020.

119. The cost of a 48–54-square-meter flat in the city is cost approximately ₮88 million ($31,000), while the land price for a 500-square-meter plot is between ₮20,000,000 ($6,980) in the outskirts of Ulaanbaatar and ₮290,000,000 ($101,270) in the center. The majority of residents (82 percent) were in debt by over ₮1 million ($355) from pension, salary, or other bank loans. Apartment and land prices in December 2021 and January 2022 found on http://www.1001.mn and https://www.unegui.mn. Resident debt data from the Asia Foundation (2020).

120. Gerelmaa Gerelsaikhan. "Mongolia Real Estate Report 2017," Asia Pacific Investment Partners LLC. 2017.

121. Of the 25 people living in a house, only 2 have an indoor toilet and 3 have an indoor shower. The Asia Foundation, 2020.

122. The average thickness of insulation for ger district homes is 35–60 millimeters of expanded polystyrene (EPS) or wool, which does not meet the minimum standard set by the Switch Off Air Pollution Project. Building Energy Efficiency Center, Mongolian University of Science and Technology, "Qualification of Existing Habitat and Heating Sources, Switch Off Air Pollution," Mongolia, 2018.

123. In 2010, the World Bank has reported that 85 percent of ger district residents use wood or coal-burning stoves for heating, See Takuya Kamata, James Reichert, Tumentsogt Tsevegmid, Yoonhee Kim, and Brett Sedgewick. Managing Urban Expansion in Mongolia. World Bank. Washington DC. License: Creative Commons Attribution CC BY 3.0 IGO. 2010.

124. Based on the data that we have collected from 12 ger district households between January 2020 and January 2021, a ger used a monthly average of 376 kilograms of coal briquettes whilst the average amount used in a baishin was 452 kilograms.

125. For houses that were built within the last five years, when taking inflation and year built into account, the construction cost is equivalent to approximately ₮21 million ($7,460) or ₮426,912 ($152) per square meter. The Asia Foundation, 2020.

126. Nicola Davison, "Out of steppe: the $28bn plan to modernise Mongolia's Ulan Bator," The Financial Times, January 23, 2015.

127. The cost to dig a well to reach the aquifer would be in the region of ₮10,000,000 to ₮12,000,000 ($3,500 to $4,200). Discussion with Odgerel Gansukh (ger district resident and local business owner, in Songino Khairkhan 43) on September 19, 2019.

128. The cost for photovoltaic (PV) panels to cover TV, lighting and appliances would cost approximately ₮9,750,000. This is 8.4 times more than the average monthly income of ₮1,157,500. This excludes heating, which throughout the winter months requires the most amount of electricity. For PV panels to fully cover the heating demand for a ger it would require 600 square meters of PV panels, and an investment of ₮166 million ($57,800). Energy consumption baseline figures from correspondence with XacBank November 23 2018, and costs for PV panel installation from mdb solutions, a local Mongolian company that supplies and installs PV panels, https://www.mdb.solutions.

129. Zul-Erdene Sharavjamts and Urangua Shagdar, 2016. Interview by Dulguun Bayasgalan, for the short film "Ger District Portraits", first shown at the 15th Venice Architecture Biennale, "Reporting from the Front", Venice, Italy, May 2016.

130. The electrical costs were ₮84,400 per month, or ₮1,590 per square meter on average for the winter (November 2018–March 2019). This compares to an average electrical consumption of approximately ₮1,660 per square meter during winter for a typical ger household, based on data collected from residents of the Ger Plug-In and a ger household in Songino Khairkhan 43.

131. Each household uses on average 3.8 tons per year, total coal consumption equalling 937,840 tons. If reduced to 0.27 tons per household the total would equal 66,636 tons, a reduction of 871,204 tons. The total number of ger-district households is based on the 2020 figure of 411,420 total households in Ulaanbaatar, with around 60 percent living in ger districts. National Statistics Office of Mongolia, "2020 Population and Housing Census of Mongolia, National Report", The Number of Households, by Type of Dwellings, Aimags and the Capital, 2020, Mongolia, 2020.

132. Meeting with the Mongolian Sustainable Finance Association (also known as ToC), between Naidalaa Badrakh, Enkhlin Davaajav, Oyungerel Munkhbar, and author on 22 October 2018.

133. Meeting with XacBank, between Greg Zegas and author on October 24, 2018.

134. Each available product is a single-story house costing between $20,700 and $27,200 and ranges in area from 38.8 to 60 square meters. See XacBank Energy Efficient Loan, Approved Construction Companies for Energy-Efficient Homes. Viewed May 21, 2021, https://www.xacbank.mn/product/1142.

135. "GIZ, A healthier home environment," BBC Storyworks, https://www.bbc.com/storyworks/humanising-energy/a-healthier-home-environment, Viewed on January 28 2022.

136. Based on a survey commissioned to the Asia Foundation, only 4 percent (2 of 45) of ger district residents have experience with mortgages or construction loans, 2020.

137. Interview with Sanchir Batbold, resident of Songino Khairkhan 43, by Minjmaa Enkhbat on 21 November 2021.

138. B. Kherlen, "Prices for construction materials increased by 52-92 percent," 12 October 2021, Viewed on January 25 2022, http://www.shuud.mn/a/534252.

139. Ibid.

140. Barry Bergdoll, et al. "Home Delivery: Viscidities of a Modernist Dream from Taylorized Serial Production to Digital Customization." Home Delivery Fabricating the Modern Dwelling, The Museum of Modern Art, New York, 2008, pp. 12–25.

141. "Boklok Skanska & IKEA." BoKlok, https://www.boklok.com/global/. and "Muji

Hut." MUJI, https://www.muji.com/jp/mujihut/en.html.

INCREMENTAL URBAN STRATEGY

TRANSFORMING AND UPGRADING THE GER

142. Asian Development Bank. "Mongolia: Ulaanbaatar Green Affordable Housing and Resilient Urban Renewal Section Project." (Manila: Asian Development Bank 2018). Accessed August 11, 2020, https://www.adb.org/sites/default/files/project-documents/49169/49169-002-pam-en.pdf.

143. The Asia Foundation, "Incremental Development Manual: Demonstrating a Model for Ger District Upgrading Market Research Report" by Munkhshur Erdenebat, Delgermaa Lkhagvasuren, and Zachary Conn, (Ulaanbaatar 2020) http://rufwork.org/grafiken/Mongolia/RUF_Ger%20Plug-In%20Market%20Research%20Report.pdf.

144. Asian Development Bank, "Ulaanbaatar Urban Services and Ger Areas Development Investment Program, Final Report, Volume I—Main Report," (Manila: Asian Development Bank, 2013). http://www.ub-subcenter.mn/webdata/upload/3006a6659f834d5710455851ba7e04e7.pdf.

145. Erdenebat, "Incremental Development Manual: Demonstrating a Model for Ger District Upgrading" Market Research Report

146. Based on data that we have collected through drone surveys of Songino Khairkhan 43 in 2019, where 361 plots out of 594 have a house on them.

147. J. Bolchover, "Incremental Urbanism: Ulaanbaatar's Ger Settlements." http://rufwork.org/grafiken/Jan19_RUF_Incremental%20Urbanism_Final%20Report.pdf2018. Research Grants Council of the Hong Kong Special Administrative Region (Project No. 17613415). See also Ger District Life, pp.53–71.

148. Based on the feasibility report conducted by environmental consultants WindMagics in 2020. "WindMagics, Feasibility Report on Environmental & Energy Consultation," HKU-Ger Plug-In Project—Mongolia, (Hong Kong, 2020).

149. Asian Development Bank. "Mongolia: Ulaanbaatar Green Affordable Housing and Resilient Urban Renewal Section Project." (Manila: Asian Development Bank 2018. https://www.adb.org/sites/default/files/project-documents/49169/49169-002-pam-en.pdf.

150. For example, although heat pumps are suitable for use in Mongolia due to the proximity of heat resources to the ground surface, the upfront costs of construction and installation are very high. With an estimated cost of $96,000 for 16 households, it would not be financially efficient unless for a scale of at least 120 households. (WindMagics, 2020, 2021) .

151. "Over the last 10 years, the incidence of respiratory diseases in Mongolia increased alarmingly, including a 2.7 fold-increase in respiratory infections per 10,000 population." National Center for Public Health and UNICEF, 2018. Mongolia's Air Pollution Crisis: A call to action to protect children's health, National Center for Public Health, Ulaanbaatar, Mongolia, 2018.

152. In 2019, UNICEF conducted a study to assess the direct and indirect costs to private sector companies, as well as individual employee costs associated with absenteeism due to air pollution in Ulaanbaatar, Mongolia: "Annual individual employee direct costs related to illness caused by air pollution totalled 875,000 Mongolian tugriks (MNT) ($317.60) for an average of three instances of three-day illness-related absences during the winter in Ulaanbaatar … Individual indirect cost equated to the median value of lost wages for a three-day absence, amounting to 120,000 MNT. The costs to employees may amount to as much as 10 per cent of annualized income." (United Nations Children's Fund (UNICEF), May 2020, Costs of Absenteeism dur to Air Pollution among Private Sector Companies in Ulaanbaatar, Mongolia, Research Report, UNICEF, Ulaanbaatar, Mongolia, 2020. https://www.unicef.org/mongolia/media/2926/file/UNICEF-Absenteeism-ENG-final.pdf.

153. Wakely, Patrick & Riley, Elizabeth. The Case for Incremental Housing, Cities Alliance Policy Research and Working Papers Series no. 1,|June 2011.

154. Ibid. "In the Parcelles Assainies project in Dakar, the World Bank's Project Completion Report found that for every US$1 of Bank money provided, US$8.2 of private funds were invested on-site." Referenced from Rowbottom, S. 1990. "Senegal Case Study, Parcelles Assainies: From Project to Place—After Three Decades." CHF Occasional Paper, International Development Matters: Framing a New Perspective on Urban Development: Back to the Future, volume 3, CHF International, June.

155. J. F. C. Turner, 1976. Housing by People. London: Marion Boyars.

156. Patrick Wakely, and Elizabeth Riley, The Case for Incremental Housing, Cities Alliance Policy Research and Working, Papers Series no. 1, June 2011.

157. Jones, Branwen Gruffydd. "Bankable Slums': the global politics of slum upgrading". Third World Quarterly, Vol. 33, No.5, 2012. pp.769–789.

158. For example, the annual interest rate on a 10-year fixed mortgage to purchase in the UK would range from 2.28 to 3.00 percent, while in Mongolia it is between 6 and 16.8 percent, depending on the type of house or apartment being purchased. Rates from Barclays (UK) and Golomt Bank (Mongolia) Accessed on April 27, 2022.

159. See "Communities over commodities: people-driven alternatives to an unjust housing system," Homes for all Campaign of Right to the City Alliance, March 2018.

160. For example, the Federacion Uruguaya de Cooperativas de Vivienda por Ayuda Mutua (FUVCAM) was assisted by Institutes of Technical Assistance and supported by the national government through loans and tax exemptions. See J. Barenstein, and M. Pfister, 2019. The Professionalization of a Social Movement: Housing Cooperatives in Uruguay. Built Environment (London. 1978), 45(3), pp 382–397.

FRAMEWORK AS A METHOD

161. Michael Sorkin elaborates the progressive shift in values from the formation of urban design and its modernist underpinnings to New Urbanism: Michael Sorkin. "The End(s) of Urban Design" in Alex Krieger, and William S. Saunders, eds. Urban Design. 2009. The University of Minnesota Press, Minneapolis.

162. Eric Mumford, "The Emergence of Urban Design in the Breakup of CIAM," in Alex Krieger, and William S. Saunders, eds. Urban Design. 2009. The University of Minnesota Press, Minneapolis.

163. The first degree in Urban Design was established at Harvard by Joseph Lluís Sert in 1960. See in Alex Krieger, and William S. Saunders, eds. Urban Design. 2009. The University of Minnesota Press, Minneapolis.

164. Both Lewis Mumford and Jane Jacobs, writing in the late 1960s, positioned the need for planners and architects to move away from wholesale demolition and redevelopment of neighborhoods into more grassroots, community-based strategies: Lewis Mumford, 1968. The Urban Prospect. Brace Harcort, & World, Inc. New York.

165. See Saskia Sassen, 1991. The global city: New York, London, Tokyo. Princeton, N.J.: Princeton University Press.

166. Neil Brenner, and Christian Schmid, 2014. "Planetary urbanization" in N. Brenner, ed. Implosions/Explosions: Towards a Study of Planetary Urbanization. Jovis Verlag GmbH, Berlin.

167. E. Soja, 2014. My Los Angeles : From urban restructuring to regional urbanization. Berkeley: University of California Press.

168. Easterling, Keller. 2014. Extrastatecraft: the power of infrastructure space. Verso

169. https://www.blackrock.com/corporate/literature/annual-report/blackrock-2020-annual-report.pdf.

170. United Nations Conference on Trade and Development, 2020. (rep.). Total and urban population. Geneva.

171. Ibid.

172. International Energy Agency, 2021. (rep.). Financing Clean Energy Transitions in Emerging and Developing Economies. Indianapolis.

173. Global Alliance for Buildings and Construction, International Energy Agency and the United Nations Environment Program, 2019. (rep.). 2019 Global Status Report for Buildings and Construction.

174. International Finance Corporation, World Bank Group, 2019. "Green Buildings: A Finance and Policy Blueprint for Emerging Markets." https://www.ifc.org/wps/wcm/connect/a6e06449-0819-4814-8e75-903d4f564731/59988-IFC-GreenBuildings-report_FINAL_1-30-20.pdf?MOD=AJPERES&CVID=m.TZbMU.

175. International Energy Agency, 2021. (rep.). Financing Clean Energy Transitions in Emerging and Developing Economies. Indianapolis.

176. For example, the Pritzker Prize was awarded to Alejandro Aravena in 2016 and Francis Kéré in 2022, in recognition of their significant contribution to architecture through their work in developing countries.

177. P. Land, 2021. The Experimental Housing Project (PREVI), Lima - Design and Technology in a New Neighborhood (1st ed.). University of Los Andes in Bogota (Uniandes).

178. See chapter 3 on Prototyping, p. 72 and Rafael Moneo, 1978. "On Typology", Oppositions 13.

179. Tom Avermaete, 2005. Another modern: the post-war architecture and urbanism of Candilis-Josic-Woods. Rotterdam: NAi.

180. Cedric Price, 2003. Cedric Price: the square book. Chichester, West Sussex: Wiley-Academy.

181. J. Bolchover, and Shumon Basar, 2005. "Demolition Hulme: Myth and Modernization" in Shrinking Cities Volume 1: International Research, Oswalt. P. ed. Hatje Cantz Verlag, Germany.

182. Oswald Mathias Ungers et al. 1978. Cities within the City: Proposal for the Sommer Akademie. Lotus 19: 82.

183. Jonathan Hughes, and Simon Sadler. 2000. Non-plan: essays on freedom participation and change in modern architecture and urbanism. Oxford: Architectural Press.

184. Fumihiko Maki, 1964. Investigations in collective form. St. Louis: School of Architecture, Washington University.

185. Andrea Branzi, 2006. "Weak and diffuse modernity: the world of projects at the beginning of the 21st century". Milan, Italy: Skira.

ACKNOWLEDGMENTS

This project is indebted to a group of highly dedicated individuals committed to improving life in the ger districts. Without their determination, patience, grit, and resolve nothing would have been possible. They are Badruun Gardi, Enkhjin Batjargal, Dulguun Bayasgalan, Odgerel Gansukh, Erdembileg Nemekhbaatar, Dulguun Batkhishig, and Uurtsaikh Sangi. In particular, I would like to thank Badruun and Enkhjin for their collaboration and intellectual contribution which has been always inspiring, insightful, and critically productive. Maintaining a sense of humour throughout, they have become good friends. Recognition should also go to the team at Rural Urban Framework at the University of Hong Kong, to the students from HKU and Columbia, and to all the local ger district residents who have participated and contributed to the collective effort of this project. Special thanks are also reserved for Jersey Poon who, since her master's thesis project, has worked tirelessly to keep the project advancing to achieve its ambitions. Additionally, I would like to thank Luke Studebaker for his careful editing and Thomas Dahm for the graphic design. I would also like to acknowledge the support of my wife Jessica Pyman who first encouraged me to visit Mongolia and to my parents, Jonathan and Joyce Bolchover, who instilled in me that architecture is, and remains, a social project.

BECOMING URBAN: THE MONGOLIAN CITY OF NOMADS

Author: **Joshua Bolchover**
Senior Researchers: **Jersey Poon, Kent Mundle**
Researchers: **Antoine Barjon, Johnny Cullinan, Minjmaa Enkhbat, Irgel Enksaikhan, Shivina Harjani, Matthew Hung, Yan Qian, Teresa Lai, Tanya Tsui**
Graphic designer: **Thomas Dahm**
Editor: **Luke Studebaker**
Main Collaborators: **Badruun Gardi, Enkhjin Batjargal**
Filmmaker: **Dulguun Bayasgalan**

DISTRICT DEVELOPMENT UNIT LTD. (Hong Kong)

Director: **Joshua Bolchover**
Project Architect: **Jersey Poon**
Research and Development: **Kent Mundle**

ENERGY EFFICIENT DESIGN BUILD LLC. (Mongolia)

CEO and cofounder: **Dulguun Batkhishig**
Cofounder: **Erdembileg Nemekhbaatar**
Cofounder: **Joshua Bolchover**
Team: **Jersey Poon, Minjmaa Enkhbat**

INCREMENTAL DESIGN MANUAL

Design: **Joshua Bolchover**
Date: **2019–22**
Project Lead: **Jersey Poon**
Project Team: **Minjmaa Enkhbat, Kent Mundle**
Funding: *Incremental Development Manual: Demonstrating a Model for Ger District Upgrading* (Project No. 17603119) funded by the **Research Grants Council of the Hong Kong Special Administrative Region**

WASTE COLLECTION POINTS

Design: **Joshua Bolchover** (Rural Urban Framework, The University of Hong Kong)
Date: **2014–15**
Project Team: **Matthew Hung, Yan Qian, Shivina Harjani, Johnny Cullinan**
Client: **The Asia Foundation, Mongolia** and **The Mayor's Office**, Ulaanbaatar, Mongolia
Design Institute: **Toonto Grand**

GER PLUG-IN 1.0
Design: **Joshua Bolchover**
Date: **2016–17**
Project Team: **Ben Hayes, Jersey Poon, Matthew Hung**
Commissioning Donor: **Lorinet Foundation**
Additional Donors: *Incremental Urbanism: Ulaanbaatar's Ger Settlements* (Project No. 17613415) funded by the **Research Grants Council of the Hong Kong Special Administrative Region.**
Contractor: **ZAG Engineering Group LLC**
Collaborator and workshop host: **IET Mongolia**
Residents: **Zul-Erdene Sharavjamts, Urangua Shagdar**
Students: **Yip Sui Yu, Chan Yuet Sum, Chen Buran, Pang Ringo, Yiu Tsz Him, Li On Yee, Lau Cheuk Hin Lincoln, Chui Tsun Yee, Yu Lingyin, Lau Cheuk Fung, Ho Sze Yin, Chui Jessie Alison, Kong Sze Wai Justin, Lee Bing Him, Wong Timothy Chum-Hin, Wong Tsz Yuet, Liu Yiding, Tsui Yan Yan, Yu Lingyin**

GER INNOVATION HUB
Design: **Joshua Bolchover** and **John Lin** (Rural Urban Framework, The University of Hong Kong)
Date: **2018–20**
Project Lead: **Jersey Poon**
Project Team: **Chiara Oggioni**
Project Partner: GerHub: **Badruun Gardi and Enkhjin Batjargal**; Ecotown NGO: **Odgerel Gansukh**
Wood Supplier: **Shinest Co. LTD**
Environmental Consultant: **Chad Mckee**
Funding: **Hong Kong Jockey Club Charities Trust** (as part of the Jockey Club HKU Rural-Urban Design Project), **YPO ASEAN United**
Supporting Institutions: **The University of Hong Kong, HKU School of Professional and Continuing Education**
Students: **Chan Hin Hung, Chan Shu Man, Chan Yuen Shing, Chang Chun Hong Gordon, Chang Lok Him , Cheung Sum Yi Dylan, Cho Quentin, Cho Tsun Shing, Chung Bing Tsun, Ho Jun Yin, Ko Chin Wang, Lai Hiu-lam Natalie, Lai Shu Fun, Lau Hio Lam, Lau Nicholas Clarence, Lee Sum Yu, Li Chung Yan, Li Wing Ho, Lin Yingying, Lo Chui Ha Jessica, Ma Kwun Ho Marco, Ming Yujie, Ng Pan Chi, Poon Wing Ho, Pu Chunpeng, Sze Ho Fung, Tam Kim To, Tang Sin Yi, Tang Siu Yeung, Tong Ka Hei Surin, Wong Gracia Yue Yee, Wong Ho Yuk, Wong Suet Ying, Wu King Tim, Yau Kai Shing, Yeung Hin Lun, Yip Shan Shan, Yiu Hin Lok, Yu Yat Shun**

IMAGE CREDITS
All images are courtesy of **Joshua Bolchover** and **Rural Urban Framework** unless otherwise stated.
Film Stills: **Dulguun Bayasgalan**
Archival Image: Photos of city buildings supplied by the **Archives for Cinema, Photography and Sound Recording.** Reproduced with permission from the director of general authority for archives @ **General Authority for Archives of Mongolia**, under legislation A/25, 2021. 4. 4.20. МУ, УТА, Х-1, Д-1

FUNDING SOURCES
Incremental Urbanism: Ulaanbaatar's Ger Settlements (Project No. 17613415) and *Incremental Development Manual: Demonstrating a Model for Ger District Upgrading* (Project No. 17603119) funded by the **Research Grants Council of the Hong Kong Special Administrative Region**
Peripheral Urbanism: The Transformation of Ulaanbaatar funded by **Seed Funding for Basic Research, The University of Hong Kong**
Green Affordable Housing Prototype for Mongolia: The Ger Plug-In 2.0 and *Ger Innovation Hub* funded by the **HKU Knowledge Exchange Fund** granted by the University Grants Committee of the Hong Kong Special Administrative Region
The Department of Architecture Publication Fund, The University of Hong Kong

COLOPHON
Published by Applied Research and Design
Publishing, an imprint of ORO Editions.
Gordon Goff: Publisher

www.appliedresearchanddesign.com
info@appliedresearchanddesign.com

Author: **Joshua Bolchover**
Senior Researchers: **Jersey Poon, Kent Mundle**
Book design: **Thomas Dahm**
Editor: **Luke Studebaker**

First Edition

ISBN: **978-1-954081-06-2**

Color Separations and Printing: **ORO Group Inc.**
Printed in China

AR+D Publishing makes a continuous effort
to minimize the overall carbon footprint of its
publications. As part of this goal, AR+D, in
association with Global ReLeaf, arranges to plant
trees to replace those used in the manufacturing of
the paper produced for its books. Global ReLeaf is
an international campaign run by American Forests,
one of the world's oldest nonprofit conservation
organizations. Global ReLeaf is American Forests'
education and action program that helps individuals,
organizations, agencies, and corporations improve
the local and global environment by planting and
caring for trees.